Praise for
Tame the Primitive Brain

"If you keep on doing what you do you'll keep on getting what you've got—that's never been a problem for me as a confirmed masochist—but for the rest of you, this book offers a clear, concise and above all entertaining way to take control."

—Tim Fountain, notoriously depraved
egomaniac and author of *Rude Britannia*

"If you think you're highly evolved and easily able to manage your reactions and emotions, think again. Mark Bowden combines thoroughly researched and accessibly presented science with real-world examples from a wide range of business situations to create a highly readable and practical system for understanding and working with your lizard brain to radically improve your effectiveness at work. *Tame the Primitive Brain* is now on the "must-read" list for all of my executive clients."

—Karen Wright, leader in the field of corporate
coaching and author of *The Complete Executive:
The 10-Step System for Great Leadership Performance*

"*Tame the Primitive Brain* is a fascinating book because it not only provides valuable insight into how your brain works in different situations, but also gives practical advice on how to communicate with and manage your reactions to others. If you want to be successful in your business and personal relationships, buy this book now!"

—Victoria Stilwell, canine behavioral
expert and author of *It's Me or the Dog*

"*Tame the Primitive Brain* is enormously practical, humorous, relevant, and accessible. You have laid out the red carpet for anyone who has an interest in growing past the implications and consequences of automatic behavior in the workplace, both their own and from those around them."

—James DeStephanis, Instructor, Self-Development
Lab, Joseph L. Rotman School of Management

TAME THE PRIMITIVE BRAIN

28 Ways in 28 Days to Manage the Most Impulsive Behaviors at Work

MARK BOWDEN

WILEY

John Wiley & Sons, Inc.

Library of Congress Cataloging-in-Publication Data:

Bowden, Mark, 1970-
  Tame the primitive brain : 28 ways in 28 days to manage the most impulsive
behaviors at work/Mark Bowden.
    p. cm.
  Includes bibliographical references.
  ISBN 978-1-118-43698-1 (cloth); ISBN 978-1-118-56690-9 (ebk);
  ISBN 978-1-118-56673-2 (ebk); ISBN 978-1-118-56650-3 (ebk)
  1. Social institutions. 2. Social systems. 3. Human behavior. I. Title.
HM826.B69 2013
  306—dc23

                                                                        2012041637

Printed in the United States of America

10 9 8 7 6 5 4 3 2 1

To Tracey:

For wrangling my impulsive behavior at work,
along with that of our tribe's at home.

I love you

Contents

Acknowledgments

A huge thanks, first, to all my family, friends, and colleagues who have helped in their various ways to corral this book into something unique and to be proud of—most especially: Bruce Van Ryn–Bocking for your expertise, insight, and supportive input; Tracey Thomson, for your brilliant ideas and guidance throughout every stage of this process; and Michael Bungay Stanier and Michael Leckie, who are the most resplendently well-humored colleagues one could hope for to whitewash this fence. Thanks also to: Shaun Prendergast, you are the stuff of legend; Den, your genius is a constant guide; Jennifer La Trobe, for your opinions and care and always being there (for whatever reason or none at all); Dan Trommater and Daniel Tomlinson, for your knowledge of the solid and the ephemeral; Toni Grates, for Namaste Bitches; Michael Turnbull, for your hair and approach to design; Rodd Olmstead, Jaime Almond, Adam Green and James DeStephanis, for your input and generous beta testing; and Ian Young, for being a winner.

I am grateful, as well, to my literary agent, Carolyn Forde, at Westwood Creative Artists, and to Adrianna Johnson, Christine Moore, and Lauren Freestone at Wiley, for their focused advice, unwaveringly positive attitude, and what has, at times, felt to me like fanatical support.

To Mum and Dad, Ann, Helen, and David "The Bad Dogg" Bowden, thanks for buying me all those *Asterix the Gaul* books so that René Goscinny and Albert Uderzo could help me to !@#$ing read and write.

To Thomas, Jack, Emily, Daniel, Peter, Robert, Steve, and Hannah, thanks for coming by every time I am home in England.

Finally, to my children Lex and Stella: Thank you both for asking what I am writing, and being interested in hearing about my book about dinosaurs, brains, and making friends. I love you both and hope you will both read this book one day.

Preface

I have been thinking, speaking about, and researching the primitive brain for many years now. Some people say that I am an expert in the field. Be that as it may, I'd like to give "a shout out" to my friend and coworker Bruce Van Ryn–Bocking as someone whose own expertise in this same area has really expanded my understanding as to why people often behave in the impulsive ways they do. A number of the most important ideas in this book were directly influenced by him.

I first met Bruce after giving one of my keynote speeches about body language; my purpose was to help a business audience understand how our primitive reptilian brain instantly judges others as to whether they are friendly and trustworthy, or not, based only on nonverbal communication. Bruce came up to me afterward and said, "Hi. That was great! I use the lizard-brain in my work, too." There was a connection.

Ever since, he and I have enjoyed working together and talking about evolutionary psychology and neural architecture, impulsive behaviors at work, and how to manage them. I always enjoy hearing what he has to say, for after years of education, training, and experience in the field, he has developed some really great ways to explain it all. At the same time, he is highly complimentary about my experiences, and how I explain them—and, of course, that's nice, too!

Although we come from different places, were born into different generations, and originally worked in different professions before arriving in this field, we work well together.

Bruce and I are alike, in many ways, I believe: We are both intrigued by the way we humans behave—how our bodies and brains interact with the environment and, most especially, with the other people in it. We both love the natural world and its history, and learning how we all fit into it. Certainly, we both agree that there is a universal human nature; by this I mean that we all possess similar psychological mechanisms stemming from the evolution of our brain—neurological adaptations, constructed by natural selection over time, that have made us more fit as a species. These mechanisms have adapted to the niche inhabited by our Paleolithic ancestors from more than 2.5 million years ago, and as far back as our Cretaceous predecessors 500 million years ago. As such, the behavior these mechanisms produce is not necessarily suited to our modem circumstances. Sometimes, it is outright inappropriate! All of which brings us to *Tame the Primitive Brain: 28 Ways in 28 Days to Manage the Most Impulsive Behaviors at Work.*

In my business communication practice, clients often come to me for help with their communication skills; just as often, it turns out that what they really believe is causing them problems is *another person's* behavior. They may, for example, be finding it excruciatingly difficult to manage the people around them. Sometimes, they tell me, they get quite upset or even aggressive with others they must deal with regularly. Then they may become anxious and/or depressed about their performance as leaders.

I cannot help them "fix the others" they are talking about—*they* are not there with us. However, I can help them help themselves, by teaching them to manage their own impulsive "primitive brain" reactions to the crazy behaviors and situations confronting them.

Bruce and I love to explore and spend time talking about the primitive brain; and I enjoy as much being able to share with others the deeper understanding I have gained through those discussions. Today, by using simple tools and models, training, delivering keynotes, consulting one-on-one, and, now, writing this book, I am able to help others deal with the people who are driving them crazy. But it all starts by helping them better handle their own sometimes insane impulsive behaviors, and giving them the communication skills they need to do it.

My goal for this book is to help you navigate *your* work relationships more successfully, so that you have a much better time at work, and never again have to go home so *#$$ed off with the people around you that you feel you are working with a bunch of !@#$ers!

I know my friend and colleague, Bruce, would like the same.

Introduction

Anyone who works with other people—which is pretty much everyone—has to deal with all kinds of challenges involving human nature. Chances are that, at work, one of your biggest problems is handling the most basic behaviors of people—such as impulsive decision making, tunnel vision, and resistance to change. And that's just *you!*

My guess is you're feeling the pressure. Who wouldn't be?

You've already seen other people snap, and totally lose it. So now you're looking for a way to best tame those primitive knee-jerk reactions, anxieties, and outbursts—and help others do the same.

Perhaps you've already read a ton of books on the latest trends in how to get the best out of everyone—including yourself. You've probably endured a mass of training. And possibly you've been tested under a multitude of psychometric models, from Myers Briggs to Strength Finder and, occasionally, have consulted the horoscope in *Elle* magazine.

Yet after all the new information and insights you've gained—and despite your best intentions—you still have no foolproof understanding of why people sometimes behave "like real jerks!"

Some people are continually frustrated by the crazy antics of those they work with. They wake up every morning to spend another day confused, wondering, "Why the hell did they do that?" Sooner or later it gets to be too much and they themselves tip over the edge, hit the roof, flip their lids, or lose it in some way. You can only keep a tight lid on this kind of frustration for so long, when, inside, you are steaming like a volcano ready to erupt.

You may recognize that it is much better to keep your cool and hold in check all those erratic, spur-of-the-moment behaviors that put your work relationships and career—as well as your own and your family's happiness—at risk. But right now you realize that when things get tricky, you are not as prepared as you would like to be to help yourself and the others around you.

You are not alone.

There isn't a person alive who doesn't wonder how to tame our instinctive reactions to the maddening situations that arise every single day. This weighs on *all* our minds. Human behavior is *the* underlying hot topic wherever in the world you go. Most water-cooler chats eventually come down to: "Why the !@#$ did she say that?," "What the !@#$ should I do about him?," and "Who hired these !@#$ing !@#$ers anyway!?"

The behaviors of your coworkers can be erratic, irritating, aggressive, defensive, fearful, power-hungry, petty, depressed, disengaged, and sometimes just plain dumb and screwed up. And no amount of management training, mentorship, or zip-wire, death-slide team-building exercises so far have helped you to understand why people (including yourself) sometimes act, and act up, like this. Certainly, none of it helps you actually *do* something about it, today.

Can that change?

Fortunately, the answer is yes. It can.

But doing so will take knowing *why* we all behave as we do—what is the root cause. This knowledge is the key to managing the stickiest situations more effectively. So let's look at the real issue here.

One hundred thousand years ago, our human ancestors were part of a scarce and scattered, migrant population of maybe only 2,000 mating couples. It was a lonelier, harsher, and more deadly world than you and I most likely live in today. We humans back then were more the hunt*ed* than the hunt*er*.

Fast-forward to today, when there are 7 billion of us on the planet together, all part of a vast and complex global network. Yet one thing has remained the same all these millennia later: The basis of our behavior boils down to the inherited primitive *survival* instincts that kept our ancestors alive thousands of years ago.

Oh, and that's not the end of the story. Our primitive instincts stretch back further still—as far as 500 million years ago—even before our reptilian ancestors to those earlier organisms that helped to found our DNA and the thinking processes upon which our modern behavior is built.

Our evolutionary chain begins way before the emergence of fish, moves up through reptiles, and on to ground-dwelling mammals and primates. It ends up with us modern humans sitting in offices, meeting with one another to talk about our organizational plans, bottom lines, and initiatives for market domination, or to address the all-important question of what we should all have for lunch—sushi or pizza?

Our human brain has developed in a modular way over hundreds of thousands of years, with each newly developed part adding, over time, to what was already there; and each alteration to our environmental niche driving a new addition to make us better fit for survival. Just as in an archaeological dig, the oldest of these brain parts is located underneath and to the back, with the next-oldest bit sandwiched between it and the most recent, situated at the top and to the front.

We call the most primitive part of the human brain the *reptilian brain,* because it adds up to about the sum total of what most lizards have in their skulls. It is made up of the brain stem, which sits right at the top of the spinal column, along with some other simple units involved only in instinctive responses and reflexes, some of which are almost half a billion years old. It is simple, yet it is *essential to your basic survival*. The reptilian brain handles stuff like heart rate and breathing; reacts to threats and rewards; and is in charge of basic sexual behaviors. When you get hungry, it's your reptilian brain telling you that you need to eat something.

Next comes the part of the brain called the *limbic system*. It corresponds to the additional part of the brain that most mammals have, and is, in this respect, primitive by about 200 million years. It is made up of the structures of the limbic cortex and some other pieces that together are involved in regulating emotions and memory and telling us who and who not to connect with, care for, and empathize with. Deciding who to include in your company of friends and enjoying that companionship is your limbic system at work.

Finally, there's the *neocortex,* which in its modern anatomical state is at maximum 200,000 years old. It's the baby of the bunch, but comprises almost the whole of the cerebral hemispheres in a fully formed adult. Mammals all have a neocortex, to some degree; however, none is as sophisticated as the human one. It is conscious of itself, and able to plan for the future and use language. You are using your neocortex right now, while you are reading. (How very wise of you.)

Each of these three biological "computers" is, of course, interconnected. Yet they all retain their own peculiar economies—how they deal with things; their sense of time and space and memory; and ability to change.

For example, our brain as a whole uses a whopping 20 percent of our entire energy capacity. Our reptilian brain uses only a tiny fraction of this to do its primary job: preserve your life, which includes getting enough oxygen, keeping body temperature constant, and warning you when you are about to bump into something—or more importantly, when something is about to bump into *you*—that could be a threat.

Unlike the neocortex, our reptilian brain is not conscious of itself. It cannot make decisions about its "self" and then develop new ideas about what different courses of action it could take to carry out those decisions. It does not *feel* for the other people around it in any caring or disdainful way, like our limbic system does. It operates only as an unconscious, preprogrammed monitor-and-respond protection unit.

Our primitive reptilian brain simply receives information from the senses and sends it to be analyzed for identification. Then, based on the simple evaluation it receives back, it instantly executes a prescribed course of action. For instance, your reptilian brain might turn your head as an attractive girl or guy walks by. It might cause your mouth to water as you walk past a restaurant from which is wafting the scent of freshly baked bread. It might cause you to "jump out of your skin" at the movie theater when a dark, shadowy face with huge fangs flashes suddenly on the screen. And it could make you want to throw your chair through an office window in frustration when your computer freezes for the third time that day, with an hours-away deadline looming.

Thank goodness we have our more social and intellectual brains to help us think through this stuff first . . .

Or do we?

Well, hold on there a minute.

Just as in our reptilian ancestors, this most primitive piece of neural architecture is first in line to receive all data, and respond accordingly. It is our primary behavioral driver; in other words, it's calling all the shots!

Still, we can of course be thankful that we have our more social and intellectual thinking brain to temper our instincts as they play out.

Whoa! Hold on again.

Something happens in the brain when we're under any kind of stress—we're too hot or cold, tired, hungry, confused, pressured, threatened, or undergoing an employee performance appraisal. The reptilian brain unfortunately regards the limbic system and neocortex—the parts that take care of cooperation, smart thinking, and openness to feedback—as too costly in terms of the energy and time they need for action. So they don't get to participate. The reptilian brain claims total executive power.

Your gene pool's journey through natural selection has given you a social and intellectual brain, but both were given a backseat to the reptilian brain, which sets off quick-fire, cheap-shot, antisocial, primitive, and instinctual drives and behavior whenever the going gets tough.

Of course, since you're not under immediate threat the majority of the time, your limbic system (as well as those of other social mammals, like wolves, whales, and apes, to name just three) has the time and energy to connect calmly and reasonably with others in your family, social group, and workplace. You feel supported and you get along splendidly.

Moreover, most often, we also have the energy and resources to bring to the party the 100 billion cells that make up our neocortex. We communicate and organize with each other to gain even greater advantages. We plan and build for our futures, and for our immediate and, sometimes, global family.

But when we're under pressure or threat, or functioning under diminished resources, our reptilian brain trumps all the others. It takes full control of the situation because it has the cheapest, most efficient, and most dynamic ways of ensuring the best conditions for *our physical survival*—even, if necessary, to the detriment of others around us.

Unfortunately, you can't stop your reptilian brain from working; you'd die in the process. But you *can* counter and manage its effects—if you understand how it thinks and what gets it so excited. This understanding is the key to dealing with the most impulsive behaviors in your workplace—including your own.

Reading this book, viewing your work environment from the fresh perspective it offers, and then following the course of action outlined in it will allow you to quickly drill down into the principles of the primitive brain. You will gain insight into why people—including yourself—act the way they do. Most importantly, you'll learn how to develop the tools and techniques you need to confidently manage those around you at every level, in even the stickiest of situations.

Here is how to use *Tame the Primitive Brain: 28 Ways in 28 Days to Manage the Most Impulsive Behaviors at Work*. You will see that it is organized into four seven-day stages:

- **First,** you are going to look at *you* now, and how you see the world today.
- **Second,** you are going to examine the *relationships* you have with others.
- **Third,** you will explore how everyone works together in bigger groups, teams, and the *tribe*.
- **Finally,** you will come around full circle to find how things have now shifted so that the *new you* can more fully understand how to better manage everyone around you—including yourself.

You can approach the information presented in several ways. You might, for example, read each of the 28 chapters one day at a time; or you might choose to dip into those that interest you most; you could even digest it all in one sitting. No matter which option you choose, you'll find that each part:

- Outlines a common primitive impulse to be managed.
- Explains the simple evolutionary theory and neuroscience behind why people can do the most illogical stuff.
- Helps you reflect on your own instinctive reactions to all of this.
- Gives you the tools to manage even the most difficult situations and behaviors at work.

Ultimately, by following the course of this book, you will achieve a new level of self-awareness, which will serve to help you navigate successfully through the craziest behaviors at work, in a calm, assertive, and empathetic manner.

So what are you waiting for? Read on to begin learning how to tame the primitive brain.

Week 1

You

A First Look at Everything

> *You can't process me with a normal brain.*
>
> —Charlie Sheen

What is this first week all about? In a single word: *you.* But then again every minute of every day is, in effect, about you, because you are living it. You experience life in a very personal way; we all do.

For example: Although you didn't write this book, and can't take responsibility for the words on the pages, you *are*, as you read, interpreting those words in a very specific, individual way. You cannot help but bestow your own meaning upon them. Yes, I, the writer, am supplying a stimulus with a specific response in mind for you, the reader. But in the end, your reactions are your own.

That may sound like a bit of a disclaimer. And it is. I have taken responsibility at my end. Your end I leave to you to hold up.

This section, therefore, is not only all about you and how your primitive reptilian brain innately makes initial judgments of everything in your life; it is also about the selfsame way that everyone else's reptilian brains first see and judge their environments—the places, people, and things that exist both outside and inside of them. By reflecting, understanding, and learning some tips about how your most primitive brain instinctively operates, you will have the knowledge you need to develop the skills for managing the impulsive behavior you observe in everyone else.

By the end of the chapters in this part, you'll be able to recognize the brain's most primitive actions, reactions, default judgments, innate prejudices, moods, and motivations that activate the behaviors of some of your colleagues, and can make them a complete nightmare to work with.

Let's begin by understanding how *you started it*!

Day 1

Shared Instincts
No One Taught You to Breathe

There can be as much value in the blink of an eye as in months of rational analysis.

—Malcolm Gladwell

Today you'll tame:
♦ Your automatic response

The following is a completely true story that someone once told me about his worst presentation experience—*ever.* After working all morning—skipping breakfast and lunch—to fully prepare to give his first pitch to the senior leadership team, a new vice president of marketing triumphantly clicked onto his final PowerPoint slide. He dramatically pronounced the end of the presentation with the obligatory prompt: "Any questions?"

No response came, bolstering his confidence that he had given the audience every bit of information that they needed. He flipped the lights back on. The boardroom

(continued)

(*continued*)

flooded with light. But to say that the reaction of the senior team was disappointing would have been an understatement.

Instead of the applause he had been counting on, all that could be heard was the embarrassingly loud snoring of the CEO—who was fast asleep at the head of the table.

Awkward—and true!

But not as awkward as what followed from the VP who had presented: His face turned bright red, just before he violently hurled his laser-pointer across the boardroom and stormed out, shouting obscenities.

Luckily, the CEO wasn't awake for any of that, either.

I'll return to this story at the end of the chapter.

There are some things to which you react immediately, without thinking. You have a knee-jerk response—a reflex. Like when, on your first day back at work after vacation, you gag upon taking your first sip of coffee made with milk that has been in the staff-room fridge for over two weeks. It's an impulse to "throw-up" the unexpectedly sour-tasting—and, potentially threatening to your health—drink.

Then there are those things you feel deep-down, at a gut level, that have to be done, and done *now*. You are drawn to act—it's an instinct. Like when, after spitting out the bad coffee, you spray a whole can of Lysol into the fridge to kill all the microbial aliens you are sure must be living in it—never mind that the site-manager's birthday cake is sitting there, ready for a staff celebration. Your compulsion to "go to war" on the contents of the cooler just kicks in; you see red, grab your chemical weapon, and all *listeria* must die!

So, you've got reflexes and you've got instincts. These are the initial impulses that motivate us all to take action. But what's the difference between the two?

Well, for a start, one fact is the same about them: Nobody taught you to activate either. Both are genetically programmed.

Impulse Buying

Take, for example, your blink reflex. (This is not what happens when you pick up a Malcolm Gladwell book and buy it just because it's there.) Rather, it's the involuntary movement of the eyelids caused by stimulation of the cornea. If your blink reflex is working right, then some dust, a bright light, a loud noise, movement close to the eye, or a plain old poke to it should cause both your eyes to blink simultaneously.

The evolutionary purpose of this reflex is, of course, to protect your eyes. Just the sudden appearance of something in your vision is enough to cause the cranial nerve that emerges from your reptilian brain to react, as if you are definitely going to endure damage to your eyes.

In fact, we could speculate that *all* reflexes are designed to ensure your survival in some way.

You experience reflexes as a result of the most basic of neural processing. For example, the *withdrawal* reflex, which occurs when you pull back quickly from something dangerous—only takes a couple of individual synapses (connections between nerve cells). Let's say that you accidentally touch a hot object. The heat stimulates temperature receptors in the skin, and then a sensory impulse travels to the central nervous system, followed swiftly by motor impulses that flex your muscles and move your body away. This reaction is so impulsive that it doesn't even get to the reptilian brain, but happens in the spinal cord. Certain actions are so vital to our survival—such as stopping ourselves from getting burned—that *no* part of the brain has a chance to think about anything. Your body just reacts—and fast.

Primary Schooling

Remember when you were born?

No, of course you don't. You weren't conscious of it. That's why, if everything was working out well for you, it was a reflex that took your first breath. It was not a conscious choice you made, or even something that your mother had to teach you, because that would have been too risky. If breathing needed to be taught, then your mother would have had, at the outside, a maximum of five minutes to teach you—which is, of course, impossible. So, instead, you inherited a reflex that's hardwired into your central nervous system to do the job of taking your first breath, and most others from that moment on.

Here's how it all works: Before you were born, your lungs were filled with amniotic fluid; and, if you were born by being squeezed through your mother's birth canal, the pressure on your chest forced that fluid out of your lungs. Once you emerged, that pressure was released from the chest, and the lungs expanded, taking in air.

Prior to birth, you got your oxygen through the blood delivered via your mother's umbilical cord. That cord continued to provide you with oxygen after you were born, until the placenta detached from the uterine wall. Once this happened (or the cord was cut), then the lack of oxygen and heightened carbon dioxide levels caused the arterial blood to become acidic. This was sensed by the vessels sending blood to your brain, your heart, and your lungs. They in turn sent a message to your reptilian brain, which sent a message to your diaphragm to contract, and so expand your lungs to breathe in. Thus, here you are today, reading this.

Well done, reflexes!

Thank goodness you did not have to think or learn how to carry out that complex procedure, because you would have killed yourself trying, for sure.

So how does this relate to the way your reflexes function in the workplace?

Say someone comes up behind you and touches your shoulder without announcing his presence. Most of us will respond by being startled. Or let's assume you prefer to keep the "notification" feature of your e-mail program turned on; and although you try and concentrate on the document you are writing, your attention keeps being diverted by the little "ping" that emanates from your computer speakers whenever a new e-mail arrives. You can no more ignore that alert than you can stop yourself from jumping when someone touches you unexpectedly from behind.

Suppressing Thoughts

The fact is, you cannot stop your reflexes. As long as your reptilian brain is fully functioning it will continue to stimulate you to breathe and to perform all of the other reflexes that it controls.

Under most conditions, your reptilian brain will always fight for breath on your behalf; cause you to blink when you get something in your eye; sneeze when you get something up your nose; or stretch your deep tendons so that you do not fall over when you walk.

It is extraordinary that the part of your brain that supports consciousness can be totally destroyed, and yet, as seen in some coma patients, its most primitive parts will still cause your eyes to scan the environment and lock onto and track any moving object. However, this eye movement, triggered by the reptilian brain, could no more be considered a sign of consciousness than could a sunflower turning its "face" toward the sun.

That is the nature of reflexes; they are automatic, and initiated unconsciously. So what about instincts?

Ingrained Habits

The simplest example of an instinctive behavior is what is known as a *fixed action pattern*, a short sequence of actions that you perform each and every time in response to a very specific stimulus.

Your instincts set in motion more complex sets of behaviors than your reflexes do. But like your reflexes, you perform these behaviors without any prior experience. So, once again, instincts aren't lessons that someone teaches you, that you learn over time. They are preprogrammed in the same way that newly hatched sea turtles are preprogrammed to automatically move from the beach, where they were laid as eggs, toward the ocean.

It is only because some instinctive behaviors depend on our getting older that they appear to be actions we've learned. For instance, we commonly refer to children as "learning to crawl." In fact, it is that they have come to an age in which the built-in instinct to crawl kicks in.

A number of our most important instinctive behaviors embedded in our reptilian brains include fighting, fleeing, courting, and preparing to give birth. We'll look at some of these later this week, especially the most "famous" instinct of all: fight or flight. But first we will look at how we think when we have an instinctive reaction. For that we turn to the topic of . . .

The Unconscious Process

Out of the continuous flow of sensory input to which your instinctive behaviors respond, the reptilian brain "forwards" or distinguishes what might be important for your Limbic social brain and sometimes your intelligent critical thinking Neocortex and tells it, "Pay attention to THIS!"

Of course, a huge amount of processing is going on before it makes you aware of any of that. And you cannot tell anyone about that processing, because you are not aware of it yourself: it is preconscious thought. Nor can others tell you about their preconscious thoughts, either.

That is why, even when we become alert to something that has happened and to which we've reacted instinctively, we are often confused—what on earth is going on, and why the hell are we reacting to it this way?

In such circumstances, both we and those around us are often completely unconscious of, hence unable to explain, our impulsive reactions, and why we have behaved as we have. The brain's electrical activity that precedes an action—called the *readiness potential*—occurs several hundred milliseconds before we are even able to start reporting the desire to act.

Out of Control

It is tough to control your reflexes. Give it a try, if you relish a challenge. Run a cold shower and walk straight into it without changing the way you are breathing, the speed at which your heart is beating, or the level of tension or relaxation within your muscles. Get the point? If you need further proof, then smack yourself hard across the face with this book (or e-reader). *Now* do you get the point?

Unlike reflexes, however, instincts can be culturally or consciously suppressed—to some degree. For instance, if you are driving your car and you suddenly see another vehicle careering toward you, you will find it nearly impossible to suppress your instinct to swerve and avoid a collision. Now take the same potential collision and move it to the world of the demolition derby race-track. The experienced demolition derby driver with a desire to win can overcome his instinct to avoid an impact, and instead, ram the other vehicle head on. Yet even he will be unable to keep his eyes open for the fraction of a second of impact.

Is Work Torture?

The late English/American author and journalist Christopher Hitchens was, he said, always somewhat proud of his ability to keep his head and maintain presence of mind under trying circumstances.

When, however, for a *Vanity Fair* article, he agreed to experience the "enhanced interrogation" technique of waterboarding (now banned as torture), which simulates drowning and instantaneously causes the gag reflex and the fight for life, Hitchens lasted only a few seconds before succumbing to the extreme panic attack that waterboarding is designed to induce. It is said that subjects will confess to just about anything under such conditions, and even experience divine revelations jam-packed with "intelligence."

The most simple of mechanisms can produce tremendous stress for us humans, as well as the life-threatening panic, unpredictable behavior, high anxiety, and altered states of consciousness.

None of us, not even the most highly trained to resist, are immune to our reflexes. That's why we can expect displays of the most primitive kinds of behavior from ourselves and others when we perceive our work environment to be an overwhelmingly threatening one.

You can't so easily control your reflexes; but you can control—to an extent—your primitive instincts. Take, for example, the murderous rage you instinctually feel toward an employer who has recommended that the department you work for abandon the project your team has been working on for 12 months; and, furthermore, that your team be disbanded and its members relocated to other departments. Like most of us, you will stifle your initial impulse to leap at the boss and wring his neck with both hands. However, under extreme stress, and within a very hostile environment, the urge toward physical violence may be more difficult to subdue. While you don't (hopefully) kill your employer at this point, you might still have those thoughts, which may very well cause you to act in an abrupt, rude, and dismissive manner, or even seek later "payback" in some underhanded way.

Day One Action

Notice when you get an adrenaline rush at work—that unexpected queasiness in your stomach and muscle tension; your heart rate speeds up, your breathing becomes shallow and rapid, your face flushes, and you begin to sweat.

Unless you work on a roller coaster, shark-dive for a living, or are having a heart attack, these are quite probably symptoms of your fight-or-flight response—your body's instinctual reaction to danger—playing out. Your reptilian brain is preparing you to either run away from a threat it has perceived, or to fight it. So above and beyond some of the physical changes just mentioned, you may also feel anxious or somewhat aggressive, or both.

In what kind of work scenarios/situations does this reaction occur for you? Do you notice particular triggers for this reaction (in terms of both people and environments)?

Try to notice the same for others: What seems to trigger them into fight-or-flight mode, or to become anxious or aggressive?

You'll learn more about the full extent of your and others impulsive responses to all these situations later in the book.

Manage Primitive Impulses Today
Awake or Asleep

We humans are normally *diurnal* creatures, meaning that we are active in the daytime and sleep at night. As with most other diurnal animals, our wake and sleep patterns are controlled by the primitive brain. This is stimulated by the levels and quality of light around us, which act as the synchronizing clock for the human circadian rhythm, our instinctive pattern of getting up and going to bed.

During midday hours, sunlight has high intensity, a high color temperature, and a high content of blue light. Our primitive brain is programmed to keep us awake under these conditions. The sun's intensity, color temperature, and blue content dramatically decrease during evening hours—conditions under which our primitive brain is programmed to send us to sleep.

With that in mind, back to the opening story, about the new VP and his snoring CEO, like I had promised.

Should you, like the new VP, encounter problems keeping those around you awake and alert at work—especially when it's critical that they pay attention to you—think first about changing the light environment; specifically, make it altogether brighter, and install bluish-white lighting. (On the other hand, should you want them to fall sleep, then by all means, switch off all the lights and mumble through a deck of PowerPoint slides!)

Think, too, about managing the environment around people so that it best meets their basic biological needs, reflexes, rhythms, and comforts; consider such factors as food, light, heat, shelter, and safety. In doing so, you may find that their primitive and impulsive behaviors almost immediately become more manageable. Keep stress levels relatively low and glucose levels reasonably high (remember to eat) and you might even be able to nip in the bud the chain reaction of reflexes and instinctual behaviors, like those that escalated into an aggressive tantrum from the VP of Marketing.

Day 2

Snap Judgments
You're Always Judging

If you judge, investigate.

— Seneca

Today you'll tame:
- Your nose for the truth

There is a lot of pressure in the world of sales. The quotas that reps are required to hit each quarter can feel insurmountably high. Timelines can be frighteningly short, or alternatively, laboriously long. And the effort that goes into building relationships, making proposals, and pushing all of these factors through to making the sale can be exhausting. Under such pressure, it's understandable that even the sanest sales executive might throw a total hissy fit, or fly off the handle, now and again.

Here's a story of primitive thinking that caused impulsive behavior to get way out of hand:

Petra had been working on Sally's company's account for months when she heard the disappointing news: Sally and her colleagues had decided not to follow through on the purchase of the new Voice over Internet Protocol (VoIP) telecom system proposed by Petra. Petra just *knew* that they had decided to go with the competitor; she could feel it in her bones, even after Sally had promised her the order was "as good as signed."

Not for the first time, Petra felt that a potential client had used her to lever a cheaper price out of the competitor. "This always happens to me with these kinds of people," she thought angrily—"!@#$ing %@*&!" And quick as a flash Petra sent Sally an e-mail, letting her have it right between the eyes, digitally speaking: "You !@#$ed me over, you #$%@!," she wrote.

She heard nothing back—though she didn't really expect to.

A month later Petra got some news about Sally's company. She heard through the grapevine that during the time she had been dealing with them, they had been forced to change direction quickly, due to their key client succumbing to a downturn in the economy. They had been in crisis and had no alternative but to cancel a number of key projects—including the one Petra had been negotiating to supply. But now, Sally's company had a major new client on board, and the project to renovate the company's IT infrastructure, to include VoIP telephony, got the go-ahead—and at a much greater scale than had been planned previously.

But, needless to say, *not* with the involvement of Petra and her company.

Call them hunches, gut feelings, intuition, "the obvious"—or, more bluntly, "just the way it is, muvver-!@#$er," your judgments often turn out to be quite accurate. Just as often, though, they don't.

Snap judgments can facilitate hard, fast, and cheap action, and in some cases, save your life. That's why you make them, even when, in other cases, they end up being the worst decisions you could possibly have made.

Get Away from Her, You B#%$*!

Some organizations are totally opposed to the notion of their employees "going on a hunch." These companies suggest that rational thought is the most advanced and effective way to proceed.

In the film *Aliens*, the character of Burke represents the corporate mind-set. Ripley is the heroine of the piece, and protective mother figure. As they are about to confront the deadly alien predator on the planet LV-426, Burke councils Ripley, "Look, this is an emotional moment for all of us, okay? But, let's not make snap judgments, please. This is clearly, *clearly*, an important species we're dealing with, and I don't think that you or I, or anybody, has the right to arbitrarily exterminate them."

"Wrong!" counters Ripley, before proceeding to annihilate the alien enemy.

From the audience's point of view, it would seem that, in the end, she's totally right in making that quick assessment of the situation, and eventually "blowing the hatch" on the mother of all xenomorphs.

But how can we, in "real life," make such quick decisions with any certainty?

We're Still Collating

During every second of every day, your brain sees, hears, smells, tastes, and feels about 11 million bits of information. This equates to the average amount of data contained in about 11,000 PowerPoint slides that your senses must process every second of every day.

Of those 11,000 slides a second, however, only one would ever make it into your consciousness—where you would realize that you were "thinking" about what was on it. By the time your conscious mind had absorbed the data on this one slide, your unconscious would have processed 100,000 more.

You can see the massive amount of data that gets reduced before you can make even a quick, conscious decision—like, "Hmmm . . . donut, muffin, or scone?" And chances are you've already made the decision instinctively; thus, your critical faculty is just spinning its wheels in post rationalization.

Compare the speed of your conscious choice against reflex: If it is working correctly, then your blink reflex from stimulation to assessment and through to action should only take a tenth of a second.

Think about the last time you *consciously* made a decision that quickly!

How can our primitive brain possibly make *good* decisions that fast?

I Think It's Safe to Assume It Isn't a Zombie

Our reptilian brain uses decision-making programming that is based on factoring in *only the minimum* specifications it needs to make the safest choice.

Here's a way to understand this process: Think about how many pieces of information you might need to consciously assess what to eat for lunch. Do I want the food hot or cold, heavy or light, spicy or plain? Do I need the food to be close at hand, or do I have time to leave the building? Am I in the mood for meat, vegetables, eggs, salad; or should I head straight to dessert? Should I invite someone, or eat alone? . . . to name just a few.

Now consider whether one of these pieces of information might be more important than any other in making a good decision about what you'll have for lunch, and where. Let's pick "close at hand." What if you made this decision based on that single piece of information? Well, in this case, it would mean that at lunchtime you might open a desk drawer and pull out a cereal bar from the box of 12 you have stashed there and eat at your desk.

Perhaps not necessarily the most ideal decision. But potentially 10 times faster than weighing every single factor, and ending up eating your lunch way past dinnertime, or the next morning.

Still Haven't Found
What You're *Not* Looking For?

Even though we share our planet with many other creatures, the human body and nervous system were designed by evolution to seek out and respond to only those aspects of the environment that are relevant to us. For example, the ants living in my front yard are designed to detect one another's pheromone trail; whereas I need an entomologist to tell me that kind of thing even exists. In contrast, I don't need a traffic cop to inform me about the vehicles speeding in and around my neighborhood; whereas the ants, as they train across the road, seem oblivious to the dangers of local human traffic. You'd think if they can detect a subtle chemical trail they would also be capable of picking up the "scent" of 8,000 pounds of SUV hurtling toward them!

Like ants, we humans also detect the world only in terms that are most relevant to us. Ever notice how after you buy a new car, a make and model that you have never owned before, you start seeing them everywhere?

We are missing most of the stuff that is out there. But that's okay, because everything and everyone else is, too.

We make our snap judgments based on only the thinnest slice of information from the mass "pie" available. Given this, it is fair to say that our primitive instincts do not make the most rational decisions, in most cases. Nor are we particularly good at predicting the snap judgments we might make; or for that matter, the snap judgments others might make when they're in the same situation we are.

This or That?

Not only do we make these many judgments unconsciously every day at lightning speed, but we do so using a very binary—black-and-white—way of thinking.

Given that the brain stem is concerned only with whether it should initiate an "approach" or "avoid" response, it is helpful when all data can be quickly poured into either a "good for me" or "bad for me" bucket—all stemming from our primitive ancestors' original query: is this food for me, or am I food for it?

We use this kind of primitive thinking because it's fast, cheap, and effective. Our sensory organs are designed to sense only the energy around us that has been proven over millennia to provide the data imperative to our lives. Our most primitive—the reptilian—brain gets first dibs at this already narrow field of information, and then it quickly deletes even more elements. It whittles the information down even further, to the bare-bones minimum needed to make the decision to alert other organs of the body and brain to initiate either a move toward or away from the environment.

This system is designed to preserve life in our ecological niche while expending minimum effort. It's a system that notices movement, color, smell, touch, taste, up/down, cold/hot, and many other basic sensations that can—in the right context—save your bacon.

The system uses only tried-and-tested, fail-safe responses to stimuli. Some of these instinctual reactions are, quite literally, millions of years old.

We're All Gonna Die, Man!

Of course, in the most extreme cases—those where the data assembled by the reptilian brain indicates a dangerous situation—our response will be to automatically launch a number of physiological responses, to prepare the body for danger. These responses include, among others: increased heart rate, heightened level of adrenaline, and dilated pupils. Those responses are getting you ready to take in more data and (as mentioned in the previous chapter) either retaliate or run—fight or take flight.

If, on the other hand, the environment indicates a reward, then responses are automatically triggered to prepare the body for benefit; the body relaxes and opens up to the environment. You are ready to stay and take/accept.

We all share this instinctual system. It is there in every human body: We are drawn toward rewarding stimuli, like the look and smell of ripe fruit. Conversely, we are repelled from potentially dangerous stimuli, like the smell and taste of rotting meat.

Data comes in; and based on the patterns by which our reptilian brain detects it, we experience an instant reflex, or "knee-jerk," reaction. This reaction will physically move us to either approach or avoid—because we recognize instinctively that, in some way, we are in the presence of *something* that has a high probability to either benefit or harm us.

If you look at this through the lens of evolution, you might see how our brain's ability to make snap judgments contributed to the fitness of our ancestors. Their primitive brains decided what was out there, what dangers they faced, and what opportunities awaited; and based on that information their brains quickly instructed the rest of their bodies to react. So in the end, we are big fans of snap judgments, since they have made us what we are—alive!

Consider the quote that opened this chapter. What the Roman philosopher Seneca really should have said, instead of "*If* you judge, investigate," is "*When*" you judge, because by the very fact of being alive, you are making thousands of unconscious judgments every waking and sleeping moment of your life. Sometimes, you make snap judgments about situations for which speedy reactions are useful, even required. For example, stepping back quickly out of the road to avoid an oncoming vehicle is undeniably helpful to your ongoing survival. (Ants, in contrast, don't seem set up to give a damn in this regard.)

Of course, some snap judgments you make are not so helpful. For example, the snap judgment you make about the value of what that sales rep is telling you about the product/ service under discussion, even *as* he or she is still speaking. Maybe it's wiser to take a second or two to consider consciously whether, perhaps, the rep's product or service *really will benefit* the company.

We are no more able to stop making snap judgments than we are to stop breathing. Both are programmed into our primitive brain. The dilemma comes when we assume that those judgments are correct. Of course, some will be right on target. But, since today's world is much more complex than the black-and-white world of our primitive ancestors, chances are that we're apt to make many of these judgments before we have all the evidence we need to make a decision appropriate for today's complicated, sophisticated, and global workplace.

Day Two Action

Notice as many of the snap judgments you make as possible. Some will be as simple as choosing to move to one side when you meet someone hurrying down the hallway toward the bathrooms. Others will be more complicated, like when a direct report tells you about his or her great idea and you instantly dismiss it in your mind, all the while continuing to appear to listen with an open mind.

Notice the snap judgments you think others at work may be making about other people's ideas.

Manage Primitive Impulses Today
Take a Break

Let's think back to the story at the start of the chapter, about Sally and Petra:

When something doesn't go your way, and makes you feel crazy, before you write a nasty e-mail and press the Send button, or pick up the phone and deliver your tirade in real time, or storm around the office . . . start another task first—something that takes at least 10 minutes.

The decisions you make in the heat of the moment may be the right ones; however, by first taking your primitive reptilian brain off high alert, you will be able to add into the mix some other capabilities to help you judge rationally. Consider taking a similar approach when you think someone around you is about to make "a bad call," "a terrible error," or to "!@#$ it up royally." Don't start by informing the person that she is wrong and should not follow through; instead, ask her whether she would simply wait 10 minutes before completing the action. Telling people they are wrong, and ordering them not to do something, is likely only to inflame their reptilian brains and cause their impulsive reactions and primitive behaviors to escalate. They may find that by spending this short amount of time away from the situation, the more social and intellectual parts of their brains will have the time and space they need to evaluate the situation more clearly, while their primitive reptilian brains stand down. And when you convince someone else to step back from the job for a moment, you also gain an extra few minutes to check yourself and review your own judgments about the situation!

Day 3

Default to the Negative
Optimism Is for the Extinct

Just because you're paranoid doesn't mean they aren't after you.
—Joseph Heller

Today you'll tame:

◆ The primordial pessimist inside us all

Imagine this: An e-mail arrives for you tonight around 10:00 PM. It's from the boss. And it says the following:

Subject: see me at 3:30 tomorrow

That's all—nothing in the body of the e-mail.
What are you thinking?
What are you feeling?
What do you *immediately* start to do?

Let's review what we know so far: Our primitive reptilian brain is making many, many decisions per second. It is capable of doing so because it takes a thin slice of data from our external and internal worlds and looks for some minimum specifications within it all upon which to base fail-safe, risk-averse judgments to either "approach" or "avoid," and trigger reflexive or instinctive responses like leaning in, grabbing, fighting, or fleeing.

The reptilian brain's primary goal is to sustain a stable internal and external environment for optimizing survival—and to do it via the least possible effort. Therefore, the reptilian brain is evaluating data that is specific only to achieving that outcome.

But what does our reptilian brain do if it does not detect anything either inside or outside of an environment that it can quickly identify as safe or unsafe? What if there is insufficient data, too much data, doubt, or confusion? What happens then?

If you actively imagined the e-mail scenario set out at the start of this chapter, then my bet is you've already experienced firsthand the answer; all the same, I'm going to make it absolutely clear.

Rumsfeld

As one U.S. Secretary of Defense once said, "There are known knowns; there are things we know we know. We also know there are known unknowns; that is to say, we know there are some things we do not know. But there are also unknown unknowns—here are things we do not know we don't know."

Sounds confusing, doesn't it? And it's that kind of confusion that the primitive reptilian brain hates!

Think about it: When was the last time that you really enjoyed being confused?

I will try to break down this confusion in terms of *risk management*, since that is what our reptilian brain is concerned with, too.

We can categorize risk here into: (a) known-known risks, (b) known-unknown risks, and (c) unknown-unknown risks. Our primitive brain assumes a brassy confidence around category (a); it deals with (b) and (c) with quite the reverse attitude.

I'll Wake the President

Imagine again the situation presented at the start of this chapter: You receive an e-mail this evening from a person superior to you in your organization. It's someone who holds a degree of authority over you; in other words, someone who *matters*.

The subject header of the e-mail says, simply, "See me at 3:30 tomorrow." What is your gut response to the nature of this e-mail?

My guess is that you *automatically* assume it's bad news. You may even catastrophize about it; that is, you think of the most extreme negative reasons behind this e-mail in order to prepare yourself for the worst-case scenario—you are going to be let go because you've done something wrong.

Here is why you think that way:

The sender (your superior) hasn't indicated his intention and feeling within this e-mail; for example, there are no customary niceties like, "Hey, how you doing?" or "Good evening; hope you are doing well." There is also no indication that everything's okay, like, "No problems—just need to check some data with you," or "I need a quick chat about timelines for the project." As such, there are a lot of "unknown unknowns" in this situation pertaining to data you might need to accurately predict whether to approach or avoid the meeting. The demand stated in the e-mail has little circumstantial, and absolutely no emotional, data.

Your primitive brain is now looking to define the "unknown unknowns" at a *maximum risk level* so that you are ready to defend yourself from any instability within your environment. It does this by turning an "unknown unknown" into a "known unknown" so that it can react confidently. The "known unknown" could read like this: "My boss is unhappy with something I did." "I forgot to do something." "Someone has complained about something I did." "We didn't win that last project; but I thought he knew it wasn't my fault."

This negative outlook is the default setting for our primitive brain. Remember that evolution keeps only the useful traits. So why is this negative default setting so useful for your primitive brain to maintain, given that more evolved thought leaders are constantly telling us to "think positively"?

Crisis of Confidence

The answer is fairly simple: Millions of years of experience have taught our instincts that assuming the worst saves our lives. Imagine our primitive ancestors hearing a noise outside the cave, in the dark. Who has a better chance of surviving (and protecting their children until they are old enough to procreate): the ones who decide it is nothing, and roll over and go back to sleep, or those who decide that the noise might mean danger, and pick up a weapon?

This quick formula for "default to the negative" decision making is hardwired into our being. It's why you can bank on the idea that people will default to a negative judgment when they perceive something that they don't fully understand—like the potentially threatening e-mail from a superior. Furthermore, they will distort the negative outcome predicted toward the catastrophic. It's better to be safe than sorry, after all. And no one wants to be surprised by the end of the world; much better to see it coming and be well prepared. Then if it turns out to be just another day like yesterday— well, that's a bonus.

I Do Not Like Broccoli

The principle, then, that your reptilian brain—along with that of everyone you work with—adheres to is: *In the absence of sufficient information, default to the negative.* Remember, too, that our reptilian brains are programmed to make snap judgments. Therefore, this most primitive part of our brain has no patience to wait for more information, or to tolerate not knowing *immediately* what is going on.

Reread one more time the e-mail presented at the beginning of this chapter. There is nothing in it that rationally suggests a huge threat to you. It simply says, "See me at 3:30 tomorrow."

At the same time, there is nothing in it to instinctually suggest that there is *not* a threat. Keeping in mind that your primitive reptilian brain operates according to instinct, the instinct in this case says that when you don't know, you should predict and prepare for the worst, period.

Think about it this way: If you want to take a walk out on a frozen lake but don't know how thick the ice is, then it is safer to make the cautious judgment that it will not be thick enough, and that you'll fall through if you walk on it.

Catastrophic Predictions

About 65 million years ago, an asteroid hit the earth. It threw huge quantities of dust into the atmosphere and marked the beginning of the end for most dinosaurs. This event, incidentally, turned out to be good news for us mammals. "Every cloud . . . ," as they say.

Will another big asteroid ever hit our planet? Sooner or later, yes. But I think it is safe not to worry too much about it, unless and until those people who have dedicated most of their lives to scientifically scrutinizing images of space tell us that one is dangerously close.

I am not a great believer in the world as we know it ever ending. Our planet has been here for billions of years, and I predict it will be here tomorrow, much in the same state it is now.

It's a pattern I have seen for the last 40 years or so of my life. But, of course, I don't know for sure. No one does. And that thin slice of unpredictability is always enough to keep my primitive brain scanning the headlines for doomsday predictions and Messianic prophecies— just to be safe. Mind you, all of this flies totally in the face of my rational mind's judgment.

A mere hint of doubt can often lead us to scuttle impulsively toward the rumor mills and spiral into catastrophic predictions about the safety of our economies, industries, share prices, jobs, or sales forecasts.

Don't entirely buy this idea? Check the stock market and see what you notice about investors' behavior. No news is always bad news!

Expect the Worst

There is truth in the saying that "the only people who find what they are looking for in life are the fault finders." The reptilian brain hates confusion, unpredictability, and not getting what it is looking for. So when it doesn't have enough information to decide whether to approach or avoid, it makes things up to fill the void. It is never an optimist; it's a survivalist. It makes up negative information to coincide with its millions of years of survival experience—defaulting to the negative is the best survival strategy.

The reptilian brain always feels safer and more comfortable in unpredictable environments once it has come to a conclusion about how it will handle the worst-case scenario it can imagine. This is a "happy place" for the reptilian brain to be, because now it knows the instantaneous action to take when the sky falls in.

This primitive attitude reflects in the standard of misery your reptilian brain will keep you accustomed to; it prefers a predictable level of hardship, rather than an unpredictable level of opulence for you.

Act Today to Preserve Today

But we don't want to beat up our reptilian brain too much for its gloomy view of the world. Just imagine how our genetic line might have fared if our default setting had been to always think positively, and ignore all the risks we faced. It would pretty much have meant instantaneous death at every turn.

As we've discussed, the cost of this security system is that it will respond negatively to everything about which it has an insufficient amount of data. That means, without enough data to support a safe outcome, we respond with an impulsive "no" to new ideas; just like, with insufficient data, we say no to most new products in the grocery store, no to most shows on TV we have not yet watched, no to most people we've never met, and a resounding no to any changes to our environments or invitations to new ones.

Day Three Action

Notice whenever you think "no" today—and how quickly the thought occurs.

Notice all the times that others at work instantly say no, without seeming to take time to ask questions, get more information, or inquire about other opinions.

Manage Primitive Impulses Today
No Time Like the Present

Remember that "no" is your reptilian brain's default position. So when you get what feels like a snappy, impulsive or ill-judged negative response from a colleague, customer, or client—anyone from whom you are really seeking a "yes"—try this approach: Just say okay, and upon leaving or finishing the call, ask the person to *think about it.* Then come back later with more information and see if you can change his or her mind.

Don't necessarily take no to be anyone's final answer; and don't allow others to take no as your first, and final, answer, either. Whenever you feel an idea has been impulsively brushed away or dissed, think about asking yourself or others, what more information could I get that would help to assess this differently? Which brings us back to the question of how to deal with that nasty little e-mail that arrived from your boss at the start of this chapter: Why not send a reply, asking for more data?

Subject: see me at 3:30 tomorrow

Hey Boss,
What's up? Anything I can do for you about it tonight?
See you tomorrow.

Maybe you'll get a reply that tames your primitive brain enough to let you sleep soundly.

Day 4

Best-Fit Thinking
Square-ish Pegs—Square Holes

If it looks like a duck, and quacks like a duck, we have at least to consider the possibility that we have a small aquatic bird of the family anatidae *on our hands.*

—Douglas Adams

Today you'll tame:
- ◆ Knocking the rough edges off of everything

Back in 1994, my best friend, actor Shaun Prendergast, was offered a role in the movie *Frankenstein,* starring Robert De Niro.

Shaun has long been inspired by (and even a bit obsessed with) De Niro. So he knew there was no way he was going to miss working with his hero, even after he discovered that the movie shoot would clash with the London run of a Stephen Jefferies play he was currently performing in. His solution was to buy every seat in the theater for two nights and then cancel those shows.

But that's not the impulsive behavior we're going to focus on here.

Before De Niro arrived in the United Kingdom for shooting, Shaun got to know the film's co-star, Aidan Quinn, well. One night they went to Shaun's home, where they sat and drank and talked; the conversation eventually led to a discussion about the cultural differences between American and British swearing. It had shocked Aidan to hear one of the film crew cheerily refer to another as a %@*&, as though it were a term of endearment.

The next morning, when Shaun walked into the makeup room, he recognized his new friend Aidan from behind, sitting in the makeup chair being prepped for filming. Shaun punched him hard in the arm and greeted him with an affectionate, "Hello there, you old %@*&."

The actor spun around—but it wasn't Aidan. It was none other than Robert De Niro! Clearly a bit surprised, De Niro gave Shaun a Travis Bickle "you talkin' to me?" look, straight from *Taxi Driver.*

Nearly paralyzed with embarrassment, Shaun uttered the immortal line, "Sorry, I thought you were somebody else," and then walked away, reflecting on how much money it had cost him to verbally—albeit unintentionally—abuse the preeminent screen actor of the century.

We've already seen how the primitive brain saves time and energy by making snap judgments based on limited data. And we've talked about how the brain hates confusion. Now we're going to learn how the brain can only identify and process new bits of information based on the neural networks it already possesses. This works in much the same way as any modern computer device; its capability to identify and work with information is limited by the characteristics of its central processor. That means that if the brain is working with only a fraction of its usual cognitive power (as happened to my friend Shaun, probably due to the stress of a first-day filming, combined with a level-10 hangover), at some point the system is going to crash and burn, and perhaps around some of the most fundamentally accepted norms for civilized behavior in the workplace.

Yet setting aside how stress, loss of sleep, and too much alcohol can restrict our processing power, we are all born with a specific chipset, some of which adapts over time, but certainly not into the level of limitless supercomputer we might hope. We are all limited in some way. How do we best manage our primitive "hammer" of a brain, the one that wants to turn everything into a nail, in order to process what it knows it can pound in?

Pacino or De Niro?

We are all born with billions of neurons, each of which has the capability of forming tens of thousands of connections to other neurons. In the first five years of life, we add new neural connections at a blinding rate of speed. This allows us to begin to walk and talk. But we can only recognize and process speech in the language we have learned. For instance, if we grow up forming the neural capacity to understand and speak Spanish, we won't be able to process and so understand much when someone speaks to us in Russian. And if our repeated cultural experiences teach us that steady and prolonged eye contact signals aggression, then that is how we will interpret it—even when that steady gaze is coming from someone who grew up in a culture where it conveys caring, compassion, or a come-on.

We've already learned that the brain has little tolerance for "not knowing." Therefore, when our senses encounter unrecognizable data, our brain will search its neural connections (our database) until it finds something that looks and feels somewhat like the experience we are having; and then it assumes it is correct. For example, when we tell the executive team our new idea and one of them asks a probing question, those of us who have had experiences of failure around probing questions might assume that he is trying to shoot our idea down, when the fact is the exec who asked the question is genuinely interested and merely brainstorming about potential challenges.

Some environments into which we venture just aren't going to fit into the thin niche we feel we need, at an instinctual level, in order to be totally comfortable. With nothing in our world ever being *exactly* the same as anything else, there are a lot of "unknown unknowns" that potentially threaten our stability. What is the brain's solution to this ultimately uninviting, quantum universe of unpredictability?

Comfortably Dumb

"She looks nice."—approach.

"He sounds odd!"—avoid.

"They seem in control."—approach.

"That's wrong!"—avoid.

Sometimes you'll be talking with someone and, for no reason, all you can think is, "I don't like this person"; but you won't know *why*. You might try to fight that instinctive response, telling yourself you're not being fair, or that your impression must be based on superficial things that should not matter, because you can't actually see what they are.

The snap judgments we make often cause us discomfort; and when we view them in retrospect, we don't

(continued)

(*continued*)

understand how they fit in with our conscious world. We make them so fast, and without basing them on any noticeable logic—in fact, often they *oppose* known facts.

More commonly, I find snap judgments make us feel very comfortable *in* the moment—so comfortable that we rarely notice them as we make them because they seem like "reality," or "how it is," rather than the impulsive point of view that they often really are. Take, for example, the snap judgment that the politician we did not vote for but who won the election is "a bone-headed son-of-a-b#%$*," voted for by "imbecilic !@#$-wits," rather than "a policymaker given office by the electoral majority." The first snap judgment makes us feel superior; the second, more considered response makes us feel like an outsider in our own territory. Snap judgment: comfortable. Reality: not so much.

In fact, our snap judgments tend to fit so well with our expectations of the moment that we don't even notice them; they mainly fulfill a predicted benefit. Now and again, however, they surprise us by being horrendously inaccurate.

If the Cap Fits . . . It Must at Least Be on a Head?

Our primitive brain does *best-fit thinking* in order to make more of the world predictable and, in doing so, more stable and comfortable. It knocks the rougher edges off of everything we experience, distorting and deleting what it needs to in order to categorize, very generally, our environmental elements, and as quickly as possible.

For instance, we can recognize in just a fraction of a second whether or not something we see is an animal. This immediate, rough impression depends on our ability to identify the minimum specifications for "animal," rather than all the individual parts.

But this system can also cause a paper bag suddenly blown by the wind across the periphery of our vision to cause us to jump out of our skin, because its movement fulfilled some of the minimum specifications for "predator." And while our response is potentially embarrassing, it has proven over the millennia to be overwhelmingly lifesaving. Such a response can also be quite entertaining, signaling as it does our brain's ability to recognize an inanimate object as "alive," based on only a few data points being fulfilled; it is what allows animators to manipulate puppets and cartoon characters to the extent that we believe they are actually real!

SPOILER ALERT: *The Muppets are not real, and are not your friends. They are manipulated to look like they are.*

Processes such as recognizing finer distinctions—for example, within individual faces—take even longer because the brain has to construct an internal representation made up of many different pieces, and then match them up with the memories it has of others. Again, it is far faster to have some minimum specifications for recognizing people and then to ignore anyone who does not meet those specs in order to find the person you are looking for.

Yes, now and again you are going to identify the wrong person—and sometimes it's Robert De Niro! But only when something in the environment is totally unrecognizable by your neural circuitry will it then fall into the category of "unknown," and so put into action a default to negative response.

Pattern Recognition

The way we instinctively process the environment around us is designed to elicit a *categorical* response. In other words, we categorize the signals coming at us, and decide instinctively how to order that information into a pattern that allows us to initiate a quick response that's to our benefit (regardless of whether the pattern turns out to be what our instinct predicted it would be . . . or not).

Categorization allows us to determine quickly whether to respond with either an "approach" or "avoid" response when more complex thinking could slow us down. If the data fulfills some minimum specifications of a threat, then make it a tiger; better to be safe than sorry—even if your response becomes socially embarrassing. For example, the tiger was actually the boss's wife in animal-print clothing, moving quickly and erratically (due to a combination of Jimmy Choo stilettos and a little too much holiday-party alcohol) into your peripheral vision, causing you to jump to the side screaming, "WTF!"). Your DNA is far more concerned with not getting passed on to future generations if you get eaten by a big cat than with any career-limiting move made in front of the whole senior leadership team (who watched you lurch across the buffet table to avoid what looked like an imminent attack to your carotid artery rather than the surprise peck on the cheek and "Happy Holidays!" greeting that was intended).

Day Four Action

Notice the assumptions you make today. In particular, pay attention when you think you know what people mean when they are talking to you. For example: How soon when you are listening to someone do you decide how the sentence is going to end, and what it means?

Notice when you are reading this sentence that your mnid deos not raed ervey lteter of ecah wrod by istlef, but the wrod as a wlohe, based on what it expects to see.

Notice the conclusions that those around you jump to, without asking any probing questions.

Manage Primitive Impulses Today
At First Blush

People around you may be, to your mind, getting a lot of things wrong because they give the situation at hand only a quick glance before making a best-fit snap judgment about the action they should take in regard to it.

Here's something you can do when others look as if they are about to mess something up: Instead of telling them they've got it all wrong, ask them to "take another look at it" or "check it again for anything out of the ordinary"; then watch to see if they notice for themselves, just by taking a second look, any potential variables, other factors at play, or potential errors in their judgment.

You may find that by simply bringing their attention to an issue a second time, they will gain a more rounded viewpoint of it, see the value of it, and, thus, be able to prevent on their own making a mistaken judgment. Without you pointing the error out to them, they may recognize that the issue under scrutiny is not quite the nail they were itching to strike with their hammer.

Given all of this, what could my friend Shaun have done to avoid his fantastic case of mistaken identity in the story at the start of this chapter, and kept him from insulting his screen idol? Well, as Daniel Tomlinson, a friend of both mine and Shaun's (with whom we both worked for years until he became a master cabinetmaker, requiring a level of study, patience, and craftsmanship that perhaps neither of us could claim), says: "Measure twice, cut once."

(*continued*)

(continued)

Maybe Shaun should have taken a second look before he opened his mouth and embarrassed himself by verbally launching an unparalleled obscenity at one of the greatest actors of all time.

That said, Daniel has also told me that he likes to put a mistake somewhere in his cabinetwork. He says that the great Islamic artists, believing only God to be perfect, thought it wise and human to insert a fault somewhere within the geometric patterns of their artwork.

Consider, were it not for Shaun's error, I would not have had such a great story to tell you.

People make mistakes—thank God.

Day 5

Friend, Enemy, Sexual Partner, or Indifferent

Categories for Approach, Avoid, or Whatever

Indifference and neglect often do much more damage than outright dislike.

—J. K. Rowling

Today you'll tame:
- ◆ The elementary way you look at everyone

The following is a true story; only the names have been deleted to protect the guilty.

Nothing about this person would have hinted at the behavior you are going to read about.

He was the internal spokesperson for an international white-collar, professional services company, and had been named as emcee for the firm's annual meeting—a high-pressure event attended by a big crowd.

(continued)

(*continued*)

In introducing the company's CFO, a woman, (who, by the way, was about to be made CEO), he listed her tremendous accomplishments, with all the respect she rightly deserved, and then elegantly gestured her onto the stage.

As she walked up to the podium to deliver her speech to the 2,000-strong crowd, the emcee shook her hand, hugged her collegially, and then, with both hands, gave her butt a big squeeze, as he announced to the crowd, "Now that's a real woman!"

He no longer works for this company.

When you view the human brain through the lens of evolution, it's easy to see how its ability to make snap judgments has contributed to our fitness. Our primitive brain decided what was out there, what danger it faced, what opportunities awaited it, and quickly instructed the rest of our body how to react to each.

There's food (good); approach it!

It's a predator (bad); avoid it!

It's healthy and of the same species (good); check it out and see if it's available to mate.

It's moving but unidentified (probably bad); hold your position until further notice!

Most of the time, of course, "it" is none of the above. That's no problem; you just go on doing whatever it is you were doing.

The reptilian brain has to make quick decisions, and so must quickly classify things. To that end, it divides them into *categories* that differ starkly from one another; for example, if it is *definitely* food, there's no way it can be a predator.

Categorically Thinking

A concept is something you can think about over time. Our most primitive brain, however, needs to decide and act immediately. Therefore, our reptilian brain does not think conceptually; nor is it designed to elicit conceptual responses.

That's why our reptilian brain's processing is designed to elicit only *categorical* responses. In other words, we classify the signals coming at us and decide instinctively how to order that information: Is that approaching shape a snake, or an apple, or "like me, and sexy?"

Categorization allows for quick thinking; in contrast, the conceptualization of the neocortex would slow us down.

Wildlife

My friend and colleague, Bruce, whom I introduced in the Preface is, in my eyes, a real expert on human relationships and our primitive brain. He lives in rural Ontario, Canada, where, in his back garden, he has several bird feeders suspended from a tree. He likes to watch the birds from his kitchen when he eats breakfast in the morning.

He tells me that while most of the birds eat from the feeders, several of them—mourning doves and juncos, in particular—prefer to eat the seed that has been spilled on the ground by the overly choosy blue jays. On the ground alongside the birds are chipmunks, black squirrels, and red squirrels. They all tend to ignore each other, except for the red squirrels, which will often chase each other excitedly, in some kind of mating ritual.

All scatter for the bushes, Bruce says, when a hawk swoops low overhead.

(continued)

(*continued*)

It would seem to Bruce and I that the birds and mammals on the ground view each other with an air of indifference. All, obviously, treat the seed as food. None of the squirrels regard the birds as potential mates, but they are hot for each other. And all these creatures see the hawk as a predator.

Finally, all of them are indifferent to Bruce watching them while he calmly eats a bowl of cereal from a distance.

Have you ever noticed that when walking down a crowded street a few people attract you, and a few repel you, but that you pay no attention to the majority who pass by? This speaks to the four simple categories into which our primitive reptilian brain puts everything, including other humans, that make up our environment. These categories can be best described as:

1. **Friend:** safe, or offers a potential benefit
2. **Enemy:** threatening in some way
3. **Sexual Partner:** presents potential to pass on our genes
4. **Indifferent:** not a benefit, a threat, or a potential mate, so not important at all

Therefore, every time you meet people at work—or anywhere, for that matter—their primitive and instinctual brain cannot help but put you into one of those four categories, and within a fraction of a second. And your brain stem does the same to them. All of us make this snap judgment based on limited data and best-fit thinking; and when in doubt, all of us default to negative decision making.

So What?

With more than 7 billion human beings on planet Earth, the default category into which you are most likely to place others every time your reptilian brain meets someone is Indifferent; and unsurprisingly, their reptilian brain is predisposed to do the same.

Why must Indifferent be the default category? Well, for one thing, a tendency to see everyone as a friend is contrary to our predisposition for survival. Doing so would risk being stripped of all our resources and attacked by those few individuals who turn out to be predators, before we could change our mind about them.

Conversely, if by default we put everyone in the Enemy category, we exist in an acute state of paranoia.

Finally, if we categorized everybody by default as a Sexual Partner—well, you can imagine the results!

Fitting In

How does the brain make these classifications among all the people we encounter?

Think of it this way: How do we know to approach an apple but avoid a snake? How do we differentiate an apple (Friend; a resource) from a snake (Enemy; a threat) from Brad Pitt or Angelina Jolie (Sexual Partner; procreation)? Do we need little packages of data or pictures in our heads, one labeled "apple," another "snake," and a third "Brangelina"?

Certainly not, as that would create too large a database for us to sift through in order to find a match for the outside stimulus. By the time we had figured it out, we would have failed to eat, been eaten ourselves, or missed out on a hot date with an A-list celeb.

All we need to detect the stimuli and their matches are the *minimum specifications* within a given category, be it a certain sound, rhythm and pace of movement, a combination of colors, a facial expression, or distinctive smell. These are all pieces of information that we use to alert ourselves that something or someone most likely belongs in the Friend, Enemy, or Sexual Partner category. We need just enough of a signal to trigger the appropriate set of primitive responses to help us get out of the way of a potential attacker, or move closer to investigate further the promise of food, friendship, or sex.

You're Fit for Work

Over the course of our work lives we have hundreds if not thousands of interactions with other human beings, all of which may have numerous, and often subtle, meanings for us; yet our primitive categorization system deals only with those signals relevant to survival, mating, and social relations, simply because these are the only ones for which the correct responses will significantly improve our fitness in an ecological niche—and, therefore, our chance of our survival. Our primitive brain does not acknowledge the benefit of a broader array of categories stemming from an initial interaction. Why not? Because that's the most economical way for evolution to equip us for survival within our niche.

Take, for example, sexual signals: Clearly, if at one time in history, certain animals in a species signaled their desire for sex, whereas other animals of the same species did not, the first lot would meet and mate more often than the second; eventually, only those members of the species that made those signals would survive, and so in time all members of the species would make those signals.

That said, our primitive signals tell us to "mate *now*," not "mate forever." And since at work most of us are more likely interested in developing long-term business relationships, not having short-term sexual flings, our primal flirting signals—though attention-grabbing—can be short-sighted, professionally speaking. For this reason, getting stuck into the Sexual Partner category will not necessarily aid us in improving our long-term professional fitness.

Similarly, it's easy to understand that when a prospective client, employer, or employee puts us into Enemy category, he will be on the alert to us, hence be very wary. Therefore, no matter how we address him, even if we use words that we think he should consider beneficial or friendly, he will frame what we say in a negative context. As such, he will avoid pursuing a positive relationship with us, and resist what we have to offer him. Instead, he will view us—and everything about us—as potentially predatory.

Why Do We Snap to Flight, and Not Fight?

Our first impulse when we detect a potential predator, in particular at a distance, is to freeze. Being still is part of our flight instinct; it makes it less likely that the predator will notice us, and more likely that it will expend its energy increasing the distance between us; or it will simply ignore us.

This simple unconscious action on our part can elicit behaviors from another organism, which will then render the situation to be fixed to our advantage. That's the beauty of our instinctive impulses; they fix our problems fast, and often at another's expense.

That is why our first reaction in the face of danger is always to freeze. After all, why would we ever fix a potential problem actively—thereby risking our resources—when an "inexpensive" action such as *doing nothing* can improve our fitness for survival?

(*continued*)

(continued)

You may have noticed this primitive instinct to freeze, to become inactive, if you have ever tried to motivate coworkers, or been managed yourself, using threats or stress-inducing behaviors. Stress and threats cause us to impulsively freeze, retreat, fight, or, if all else fails, "play dead," rather than be more productive. So the next time you are tempted to motivate a team or colleague with a kick to the backside, ask yourself whether you are really anticipating one or all of the following reactions: freeze, flight, fight, faint. Because that's what the team's/colleague's primitive brain is going to give you.

Again, So What?

To repeat, we are, by default, likely to be shoved unceremoniously—alongside our message, product, or service—into the Indifferent category. So although we're not a predator, we're certainly not a resource either, *and definitely do not offer an opportunity to procreate!* Therefore, we are of no discernible use to the other human, whose primitive brain is judging us.

Simply put, this means we are neither seen nor heard again, unless and until we send the right signals to get us moved into one of the three categories that elicit attention. (I say more about these signals in my first book *Winning Body Language*) The same goes for people at work who are trying to get on *your* radar screen.

The best option for everyone attempting to create and maintain long-term relationships at work is to be fixed firmly in the Friend category, to show that we are there to assist our colleagues, to "feed" them, and to be of service in their quest for greater resources and ultimate survival in the workplace. Conversely, we want them there for us in the same way.

How do we come to believe in others and trust they can be our friends? How can we get them to see us in the same light?

Trust in Behavior

More than anything else, we humans believe and trust *what we see*. If you exhibit behaviors that demonstrate you are a friend, you increase the opportunity for positive engagement. If, instead, you behave in a way that alerts the primitive brain in others that you are the enemy, or a predator of their resources, you increase the chances that they will shut down to you. But if you come across as neither of those, others probably won't acknowledge you at all—unless of course they think you are sexy!

As popular children's book author J. K. Rowling says, and rightly so, it is indeed indifference that can cause the most damage to us in the workplace. If you are indifferent to those around you, or vice versa, your ability to work well together sinks to a level nearing zero. You simply will not even feature in their individual worlds, and they certainly won't feature in yours. You might as well be dead to each other!

Day Five Action

Notice the categories into which you put those around you: Friend, Enemy, Sexual Partner, or Indifferent. How does this categorization affect your behavior toward them?

Notice the behavior of those around you. Imagine into which categories they may be putting others (including you), and how those distinctions drive their behavior.

Manage Primitive Impulses Now
Monitor Your Lizard Brain's Categorizations

Your initial—primitive—categorization of those you work with will govern your behavior to and around them and, in turn, will be reflected in how they behave toward you.

If you are having difficulties with a colleague, provider, client, leader, or customer, it may help to identify the category into which you have placed him: Do you see the person as a friend, enemy, or sexual partner; or are you indifferent? Once you recognize how you categorize people, you can then start to appreciate why they may be behaving toward you as they are, in reaction to your categorization. Most importantly, you can then choose to put them in more appropriate categories so that they begin to respond with the behavior you would like to see from them.

If only the emcee in the opening story of this chapter had recognized his primitive brain's sexual attraction to the female leader he was introducing, along with its indifference to her powerful position in the company, he probably could have checked himself before he wrecked himself. (We'll explore fully the effects of hierarchy on the primitive brain in Part Three.)

And he probably could have managed the situation by, for example, planning ahead to restrict physical contact with the CFO to that which was appropriate to the situation; he also could have rehearsed his introduction, and planned to give her *only* a warm handshake and a friendly embrace. All of these steps—the self-reflection, forward thinking, and planning—would have engaged his intelligent modern brain, the neocortex, and allowed it to override his primitive, reptilian brain.

Day 6

Moods and Emotions
Good Days and Bad Days

When you've seen the world shape up as I have, there are only two things you can do: laugh or kill yourself.

—John Le Carre

Today you'll tame:
◆ Your temperamental nature

Greta typically had her meetings with her mentor on the first Monday of each month. Always, it would go the same way: Within five minutes, the discussion would digress into a complaining session on the part of her mentor, who would carry on about how futile business was, and the barriers she needed to overcome that week, raised by the annoying people she had to deal with. As far as Greta was concerned, she gained nothing from these interactions, and the relationship seemed pointless to her. She also worried that one of the annoying people her mentor was grousing about was herself. All in all, she felt a bit picked on.

(continued)

(*continued*)

Greta's mentor had another mentee, Boris, so Greta decided to ask him about his experience with their mentor. "Fantastic," Boris told her. "She really focuses on what I need from the work and the organization, and how I can best go about getting it. Our meetings are always very positive."

"Maybe she just hates working with me," thought Greta, despondently.

The first Monday of the next month Greta's mentor was away on business, and when she returned midweek Greta asked to see her that day for a session. She told herself that she would be brave, and during the session broach her concerns by asking, "Do you have something against me?"

This session, however, proved to be dramatically different from the others, from the moment it began. Greta's mentor behaved as a great coach and a huge help to her. She asked specific questions, helped Greta solve problems, and engaged her in a valuable discussion. Greta no longer felt like the repository for the woman's complaints.

What made the difference?

Simply, the day of the week.

Now Greta always meets her mentor on Wednesdays. Turns out, the mentor is always in a bad mood on Mondays. (And, really, who of us could blame her for that?)

Way back in our primitive caveman and cavewoman days, emotion was an automatic mechanism for shifting our behavior to better meet our basic needs. That is why experiencing an emotion doesn't require us to first *think* about what is going on. In this way, emotion has aided in our survival. It can impact our autonomic nervous system, as well as our breathing, perspiration, heart rate, and a host of other physical reactions. These physical responses are useful for changing our behavior quickly, for our benefit. If we are angry, we will have the impulse to fight; if fearful, we will freeze or flee, and so on.

Emotions also are reflected in our facial expressions, tone of voice, and body language—our nonverbal forms of communication. This is helpful for altering the behavior of others—again, for our benefit. A pleasant demeanor is inviting to others; they want to spend time with us. When we're sad, it invites compassion. Sexy invites . . . well, you get my point.

Of course, we are not emotional all the time. As we have all experienced, our emotions come and go, and sometimes one replaces another rather quickly. Even those of us who might appear more emotional than others have periods when we are not filled with any particular emotion.

We also all have moods, as well as emotions. What's the difference between the two?

Are You Feeling Blue?

We can distinguish moods from emotions in terms of how long each lasts, and how they are produced in your brain. Moods last much longer than emotions; emotions can be fleeting, and typically stick around for only a matter of seconds, or a few minutes, at most. When we think an emotion has lasted for hours, we are probably experiencing or witnessing a recurring emotion; or of course, someone who is simply "in a bit of a mood!"

Moods can last for hours, sometimes for days. If they last much longer than that, the person "in the mood" is perhaps suffering from an *affective disorder*—manic or depressive or maybe a big change in their life. Often, we can be angry for a few minutes and then irritable for the rest of the day, but then feel entirely different the next day, because our dark mood has passed—thank goodness!

In the Mood for Anger?

Moods can lower the threshold for arousing our emotions, which occur most frequently during a particular mood. For instance, a person who is in an irritable mood can become angry more readily than usual. Events that ordinarily might not bring on anger are more likely to do so when we are feeling irritable, because we construct the world around us to best fit our current mood by focusing on—and often expecting—events that require an angry response from us.

This tendency can easily be explained. Remember *best-fit thinking*, which we looked at on Day Four? Our brain uses this kind of thinking to help make our experience of the world more predictable, and thus more stable. In short, we make the data we are receiving fit *with the mood* we are currently experiencing. It's more predictable *for* us, therefore it feels better *to* us—as odd as that may sound. Remember: Our primitive brain hates unpredictability.

Moods also affect our ability to manage any particular emotion. A person in an irritable mood will not be as able to control an episode of anger as well as he could if he were in more pleasant mood. Instead, he may experience more intense anger, and that lasts longer.

What Started This?

The trigger for an emotion may be in the environment, a memory, or something we only imagine. Frequently, we may not even be aware of what provoked a given emotion; we may only recognize the cause of our reaction during or after the emotional episode.

A physical reaction occurs within us when we experience an emotion. Some of the changes—like those associated with negative emotions—are unpleasant. For instance, when we are very anxious, we may feel sick to our stomachs; when angry, we might suffer hypertension and palpitations; and when we are sad, we might cry so much that our face puffs up like we are having an allergic reaction. Other changes are a lot more pleasant: when we are first in love we may feel light and energized; when we are happy and amused we may laugh until we become giddy (from an upsurge in endorphins, the natural opioids produced in our brains); and when we have a sense of accomplishment and success, we feel healthy and strong (and our testosterone level rises—in both males and females). Whatever the emotion we are having, it will produce biological reactions automatically within us.

Now this explanation may make life sound either unromantic, or a lot less painful than it actually can be. Certainly, knowing the reason why your body reacts as it does every time you see someone attractive to you, or who looks friendly or aggressive, does not change the fact that you feel that way—and that it feels *real!* The world around you can cause a shift in your moods, pleasant or not, and here's why . . .

Change = Threat

Change is, by nature, unpredictable and, therefore, inherently "bad" for our reptilian brains, which as I've said, prefer stability and therefore predictability. We impulsively retreat from change the way we back away from a potential predator. It follows then that it is inherently difficult for humans to feel instinctively that change is good for us, and to react impulsively in a positive way about it. Rather, we are likely to start moving through the freeze → flight → fight → faint behaviors during times of change. Here's how that can play out:

1. **Change arrives.** We have insufficient data about the outcome of that change, so we default to the negative, and *freeze* to allow the predator to move on.

This freeze process can last for minutes, hours, days, months—even years! Remember, DNA and evolution have nothing but time on their hands; they have seen ice ages come and go without having to adapt too much.

How might this be demonstrated in an organization? One scenario might be that although everyone has heard that change is imminent, and stakeholders have been instructed to deal with the possible aftereffects of implementing the change, absolutely *nothing* is happening. No one wants to deal with whatever it is they've been warned to expect.

2. **Change does not go away.** We experience a threat, and take *flight* to move away from the predator. This part of the process, too, could take anywhere from fractions of a second to years. This might occur in an organization that demands or requires change, even though its employees display a clear aversion to it. So, though everyone is preoccupied with the change, they won't actually get to work on it until next quarter, next year, next decade.

3. **Change is underway.** At this stage, we continue to experience the change as a threat, and react with the *fight* response, because flight has clearly not worked. Now the predator is not only hot on our heels but has cornered its prey—us. We see this in organizations where everyone is totally resistant to the change. The stakeholders may even have consciously organized themselves into a resistance movement; however, it's more likely that there is an unconscious but powerful unspoken resistance to change.

We may very likely also notice that although managers give instructions to implement the change, their employees not only fail to carry them out but often do the exact opposite of what they're told. After all, if we inherently view change as a predator, why would we ever follow the instruction delivered by the predator's minion—management? It stands to reason in this case that impulsively executing the *opposite* of the instructions is likely to keep us alive longer.

4. **Change is underway with force, and resistance has proven futile.** Since we still perceive a threat, we opt to faint (another form of flight). Using our instinctual play-dead response may, we think, prompt others to regard us as weak, diseased, or simply not a resource worth plundering. We hope this behavior convinces the predator to move on to another victim, one that has more energy resources to spare, and no diseases it could catch. In an organization, this can manifest in a number of behaviors, from people taking sick days to being inaccessible, either by phone or e-mail ("Where *is* everyone?" They have gone dead on you!). Alternatively, employees may move around the office like the living dead—unconsciously "working to rule."

As noted in Day Five, there are plenty of business leaders who seek to motivate their teams by making threats and causing stress and anxiety; there are also many managers who seek to motivate by delivering inspirational speeches on the value of change. Regardless, leaders typically have very little understanding of just how threatened our reptilian brains are by change, of whatever sort it is.

There are many models for change that, because of their strategic level of engagement, are probably aimed at the neocortex (i.e., the modern brain, which is more than capable of the most academically complex thought). Yet until we have proven to our reptilian brain that a given change holds a clear advantage for it in terms of survival, it will continue to respond in flight-or-fight mode to enhance its fitness. To hell with the organization and its goals!

Pull the Trigger

Of course, we're not literally struggling for our lives every time we experience an emotion. Our emotions have developed over time; they've grown more numerous and become more sophisticated. Nevertheless, the most basic emotions are universal and cross-cultural. At the same time, what triggers them can be very different from person to person and from place, company, and time.

Here are a number of the most common emotional triggers for you, as an individual:

♦ You detect a particular set of "correct" signals in your environment, which indicate that an impulsive emotional reaction would be appropriate and of benefit to you. For example: You discover too late that the production department does not have the prototype for the new robot ready because the software engineers are two weeks behind schedule. Your client's CEO and director of R&D just flew in from Europe to watch you demo the new robot. Egg on everyone's face, and devastating for the reputation of the company. You make it clear to the manager of custom software how embarrassed and angry you are; you chew him out in no uncertain terms to ensure he'll never let you down again.

♦ You think about something that has happened, or is happening, and just the thought sparks feelings in your emotional database. For example: You're in a meeting with a colleague who informs you that in the future your team will be reporting to a manager you dislike intensely. This is the first that you have heard of this and you react with anger and fear, unloading on your colleague like a ton of bricks—in effect, killing the messenger.

♦ You remember a situation when you felt strong emotions. You can either feel the same way now as you did then, or experience new emotions in reaction to what you felt then. For example: You are walking to your car when you see the VP of finance getting into her car, across the parking lot. You immediately flash back to the last time you were in a meeting with her, and recall that she spontaneously praised you for lowering your department's costs by 15 percent. Just as you did then, you now feel warm and happy inside and, as she catches your eye, you nod to her and give her a big smile.

◆ Your imagination allows you to create scenes and circumstances that awaken emotions in you. It's easy to imagine what it would feel like if you were extremely happy or extraordinarily angry; and as you do this, you start to get a sense of that emotion inside you. For example: You just heard through the informal corporate network that a colleague has been promoted, and that other promotions are in the works. You begin to imagine what it would be like if you were one of those slated to get a boost up the corporate ladder; you start to get excited and even elated about having greater authority, a raise in pay, and perhaps even that elite club membership.

In the same way, it's often enough to remind yourself of how angry you were about something that happened in the past, to get angry all over again. For example: You wake up in the morning and, as usual, turn on your BlackBerry first thing. There, in your inbox, is an e-mail from your VP, telling you that the executive team reversed its earlier decision and will, after all, let your team continue to work on the project that had consumed you for the past six months. Even though this is good news for you, and you feel relieved, you also can't help remembering what idiots they were to think of cancelling it in the first place.

Just thinking of how furious you were when you heard they were going to cancel the project makes you angry all over again.

◆ Emotions have clear physical expressions, and you can trigger the internal, mental experience of having them by consciously using your muscles—especially your facial muscles—as you would if you were actually experiencing the emotion, and in doing so, trigger the emotion. For example: You are jet-lagged and exhausted from an 18-hour flight halfway across the world. After a harrowing taxi drive from the airport to your hotel, you have to go directly into a meeting with a prospective client, whom you have never met. You know that first impressions matter, and that if things go well, your company's future is secured for at least the next three years. While you can't do anything about your fatigue, you can still smile, and so that's what you do as you walk into the meeting room. Your smile helps you to feel good and the prospect's first impression of you is of a friendly soul who is genuinely happy to be there.

It's clear that emotions can be triggered in a number of different ways; and for each of these ways, there are a number of different reasons for them. Similarly, moods can be caused by all of the above. Just be aware that moods also have strong biochemical components, and therefore are at the mercy of the hormones coursing through our bodies (a topic we'll talk more about in the next chapter).

Find What You're Looking For

The big problem with emotions is that once we have one, it's very hard to think in ways that don't conform to that emotion. This brings us back to best-fit thinking. In response to an emotion, our memories, our impressions of the world, suddenly become very selective, as does the vocabulary we use to describe that emotion, whatever it is. For example, say a trusted colleague tells the boss that he doesn't think your idea will turn out profitable for the company, and you are worried that his viewpoint will prevail; you then feel justified in telling him that he "stabbed you in the back." Imagine how *actually* being stabbed in the back feels physically: much worse than someone disagreeing with an idea we have. But neurologically speaking, the feeling of being let down by a friend and being knifed from behind are both registered in the self same pain centers of the brain.

Furthermore, being swamped by an emotion in this way will prevent you from remembering facts you know to be true, knowledge which contradicts the emotion you're experiencing. For example, let's say that you become upset by the only piece of negative criticism you got in your performance review. After reading this criticism it becomes almost impossible for you to recall the numerous other performance areas in which you received praise. What you *do* remember is distorted by the emotion, creating thinking such as: "When he said that I excelled in client management, he looked away from me, so he probably didn't mean it."

Negative Thinkers Are Winners

Research shows that it takes nine positive comments from a superior to make up for one negative comment. Why might this be?

Remembering negative experiences helps us survive. Who of us could ever forget a stretch of highway, covered in black ice or oil from a spill, where we lost control and

(*continued*)

(continued)

thought we were going to die; or that episode of food poisoning after eating at that popular restaurant downtown? We remember such events vividly because our primitive brain knows they could happen again, which would be bad for us. An inquisitive two-year-old needs to have embedded in his brain that touching a hot stove really hurts. Otherwise, he might continue to touch the stove and end up enduring permanent damage.

That is why the memory of our boss yelling at us never goes away, and why it might be a long time before we let our guard down with her.

When we are experiencing a negative emotion, we're not likely to notice any positive possibilities and openings. Imagine having just lost a major contract at work and feeling anxious about how this might affect the stability of the company—not to mention, your job. Most likely, you don't start to consider whether this loss might free up the company to take on two more new contracts, and at higher profit margins. The opposite can occur, too: When you are in an ecstatic mood, you become blind to everything that does not confirm your great feelings—meaning that you are considerably less capable in those moments of recognizing potential danger. For example, assume you've been asked to pitch on a huge contract and are so excited you neglect to check whether the potential client company is solvent. In your elation you just assume that if the company is soliciting pitches, it must be swimming in cash.

Whenever we experience a strong emotion we are operating at a primitive level, and therefore not looking to challenge it; to the contrary, we tend to seek to strengthen and maintain it. The good news is that emotions can save our lives; for sure, they make life worth living, and are perhaps the essence of our humanity. The bad news is that some of them are difficult to deal with.

However we judge emotions and moods, good or bad, one thing is certain: They are not going away. Think about it; you are in a mood right now, and perhaps even having an emotional reaction to what you are reading.

Day Six Action

Today, notice whenever you have an emotional reaction or are in a mood. Which of your moods or emotions would you describe as a reaction to outside events and people; which would you describe as coming from your internal state?

Notice the moods and emotional reactions you think you see in those around you. Do you think they are related to you in some way (our reptilian brain tendency is to think that everything is about us)?

Manage Primitive Impulses Today
Emotive Decisions

Strong emotions can distort our perceptions of the world. Negative emotions, for example, can cause us to block off potentially positive experiences; they may also resurrect other long-buried negative thoughts— adding fuel to their fire.

If you are experiencing an overly negative emotion—which may become evident to you if you examine your overriding mood—better to wait until the emotion
(continued)

(*continued*)

has passed before you take any monumental actions (that you may live to regret!), even if it is difficult to resist the urge to do so.

The following is a good exercise to help you recognize your emotional state.

Think about your mood; now put it into one of two categories, good or bad.

Just doing this can give you insight into your mood for the day and give you a clue as to how you might end up acting and reacting to others.

For example, if I recognize that I am in a bad mood, I know that right now is probably not a good time to listen to new ideas from anyone. Doing so may make me irritable, or even potentially threaten me and make me angry. I know, too, that if you were to come to me with some suggestions at this time, I must recognize that some of my negative reactions may be *overreactions,* and that I either need to review the ideas later, or tell you to come back another day because today isn't the best day for me to consider new things. On the other hand, if I'm in a good mood, now might be a great time for others to review my behavior. We might all find that while in this mood I am capable of accepting potentially critical ideas, about myself and my performance, more easily and pleasantly.

Following your self-reflection and predictions, you can decide whether you might want to plan to do—or *not* do—something to make the day work out better for you and those around you.

Don't forget, however, to take into account that emotions can be fleeting, and moods short or long-lived. So ask yourself: How long do I think this mood might last? Is there anything I can do that might quickly change my mood for the better? Would it be useful to do that today?

Day 7

The Spice of Life

The Internal Environment That Shapes Behavior

F**k you, hormones!

—Ben Stone

Today you'll tame:

◆ Peptides, lipids, and monoamines (the little !@#$ers)

We never knew why, and we probably never will (since nobody ever dared to ask), but one day, out of the blue, one of the women who worked at the office suddenly pelted her full cup of coffee at the window, narrowly missing my friend Marcella's head before smashing right through the plate glass. Then she sat down and got right back to work, like nothing had happened.

Nothing seemed to have set her off, and she never explained herself afterward. It was utterly *mental*!

Or was it?

There are so many hormones coursing through our bodies, 24/7, that it would take an entire book just to list them all, with a full explanation of what each one does. But here's a quick rundown: Some of them will make you sleepy, some will make you run away, and some will make you bloat with water. Some will cause you to eat more. Some will get you feeling sexy, and some will get you ready to give birth. Some will cause you to grow a beard and others will cause you to grow breasts. Some will make you happy, some will make you sad. There are some that can reduce pain and some that will impede your immune system's ability to fight disease.

Some of the time, you may be able to control these hormones by taking medication from your doctor, or by changing what you eat, how you exercise, sleep and generally live your life. Other times, you will have no control over them. And that might put you on quite a roller-coaster ride.

Chemical Dependence

First, and most obviously, we know that moods—as we discussed in the previous chapter—can be brought on by changes in one's neurohormonal, biochemical state. And this state has a longer life cycle, or rhythm, than our emotions. So when we look into why we may be feeling a certain way or be in a certain mood, we should also consider our hormonal state—this week, month, season, or even year—and what may be causing it.

Again, an explanation of the causes of hormonal change can fill many books, but it's easy to name a few here: lack of sleep, onset of adolescence, menstrual cycle, menopause, hyper- or hypothyroidism, stress, love, pregnancy, looking for or losing a partner, competitive or supportive environments, the weather, the season . . . the list goes on and on.

More than any other, though, the chemicals that run our *primitive* brains are the *neurotransmitters*. Different types of cells in our body and our brain secrete different neurotransmitters. Impulses move through the brain along neural pathways, which are chains of neurons that secrete the same chemicals and spark one another. Each brain chemical may have a different effect, according to where in the brain it is activated.

Some neurotransmitters are excitatory; that is, they encourage the cells they come in contact with to "fire." Others have the effect of shutting down neural activity. Hundreds of different neurotransmitters have been identified, among which the most important seem to be the following:

♦ **Serotonin:** This is the neurotransmitter that is enhanced by Prozac and other similar drugs, and is sometimes referred to as one of the "feel-good" chemicals. Without question, serotonin has a profound effect on mood; those who register high levels of it tend to experience greater serenity and optimism, and those with less tend to be more anxious. This chemical also has some potential negative effects, including rapid heartbeat, restlessness, nausea, and dramatic changes in blood pressure. You can inadvertently raise your serotonin levels, in an indirect and nondramatic way, through diet.

Serotonin is derived from tryptophan, the same amino acid in turkey meat that makes everyone sleepy after a Thanksgiving meal, bringing on the infamous "turkey coma." A carbohydrate-heavy meal can also cause the body to release insulin, at which point all amino acids in the bloodstream—except for tryptophan—are absorbed into the body. The tryptophan is then able to raise the serotonin levels without obstruction. This might be one of the reasons that most people don't work well right after lunch! Regular exercise has been shown to result in an increase in serotonin levels and improve our mood.

- **Noradrenaline:** This is mainly an excitatory chemical that induces physical and mental arousal and heightens mood. Its production is centered in the brain's pleasure center. It produces wide-ranging physical effects on many areas of the body, and is often referred to as a "fight-or-flight" chemical, as it is responsible for the body's reaction to stressful situations. Noradrenaline generates physical responses, like increased heart rate, higher blood pressure, pupil dilation, dilation of air passages in the lungs, and narrowing of blood vessels in nonessential organs. These responses enable the body to perform well in stressful situations.

- **Oxytocin:** This hormone helps "melt the edges" of our minds, creating a sense of oneness with others, and so helping us forge bonds of warmth for and trust in one another—especially mothers for their babies, and lovers for each other. Women produce huge quantities of this chemical during childbirth, as do both sexes during orgasm. Oxytocin evokes feelings of contentment, reduces anxiety, and stimulates feelings of calmness and security around a mate. It also increases a sense of trust, and decreases fear.

- **Dopamine:** This chemical helps regulate movement and emotional responses. Dopamine identifies and recognizes potential rewards and then sets us into action running after them, generating desire, anticipation, and excitement in the process. This is due to the fact that a high level of dopamine in our brain promotes feelings of satisfaction and reward. It can, literally, feel like an addictive high. Our bodies produce high levels of dopamine when we eat, have sex, or complete a task we undertook to gain a reward we desired.

Ancient Humorists

My friend and colleague, the magician Dan Trommater, recently bought me a T-shirt with a couple of dinosaurs on it and a slogan reading: "SEROTONIN & DOPAMINE: technically, the only two things you enjoy."

I think that's pretty funny.

Dopamine pathways snake around the brain doing different things in different places, especially deep in the brain stem. Dopamine-producing neurons keep us going physically as well as mentally. When the brain's reward circuit is stimulated by dopamine, the body gets geared up to grab or chase the object of desire, producing the conscious sensation of excitement and fixing our attention on the goal, at the same time generating a pleasurable high.

But it is a quick hit. These sensations do not produce lasting satisfaction. A dopamine high tends to be followed by the need for another, and another, which is the basis of psychological addiction.

Dopamine is also involved in generating meaning—the feeling that the world hangs together. Disturbances in production of this chemical may, therefore, produce a sense that things are falling apart—or, on the other end of the spectrum, that everything is drenched in significance and connected in a wonderfully holistic way.

Studies have found that dopamine levels increase in our brains when we are in environments where we perceive we have more resources. These environments cause us to become excited, and provoke our approach response. Conversely, dopamine levels decrease when we're in environments we perceive to have no resources for us, which stimulates our response to retreat from them. Likewise, unpredictable environments prompt a drop in our dopamine levels and stimulate our most basic retreat response from those environments.

More predictable environments—those we perceive to be full of "known knowns"—stimulate our approach response. Therefore, we are impulsively drawn toward such environments. And environments where we feel we have a choice, or in which we perceive we are autonomous, stimulate dopamine production within our brains and can cause us to instinctively approach them, too. On the contrary, if we think that an environment gives us no choice, we are programmed at a primitive level to avoid it.

Diminished Responsibility

If we cannot escape an environment that is "bad" for us, we are left with no other instinct than to fight it. For instance, have you ever felt that you were stuck in a job; had no resources there, no promise of success, and worse, no possibility of finding another job? Thus your only option was to get angry and aggressive toward the people you worked with?

Even if you weren't consciously aware that this was happening to you, you may, upon looking back on the situation, recognize that you were indeed in that position and state of mind. In retrospect, you realize that your primitive brain at that time decided it had no resources in that environment to sustain its immediate need for survival; nor did it know with any certainty what choices it may have had regarding resources it *might* have been able to obtain. With that in mind, you can see that it was a no-brainer (excuse the pun) that you would have been unconsciously driven into aggressive behavior.

Chances are, as well, that your aggressive behavior did not serve to alter that negative environment; in which case, you may have found that you were left with only one alternative: to play dead. As we've seen, this response can manifest in a variety of forms in the professional world—anything from total disengagement from your work to taking more than your allotted ration of sick days to being unreachable by e-mail or phone to totally ignoring people who need to communicate with you.

Our hormonal and neurochemical levels are set at the optimum point to ensure our survival within our environment and ecosystem. That is, they are high enough to keep us in pursuit of what we need—such as food and reproductive opportunities—but not so high that we start to see our mortal enemies as part of a great, loving superconscience. It is these internal biological levels, in conjunction with the external environment, that will shape our mood, feelings, and how we see the world around us, not only on a minute-by-minute basis, but also for longer cycles within our lifetime.

Biologically, we tolerate only a minimal degree of variability. For example: The bloodstream is highly sensitive to its acidic levels. A slightly alkaline pH of 7.41 is ideal. Anything above or below this is dangerous. That's some pretty inflexible biochemistry right there!

Hell's Seesaw

Medically speaking, we are under stress whenever we deviate from our normal state of being, which is biologically referred to as *homeostasis* (derived from the Greek, *homeo,* for "similar," and *stasis,* for "state of balance or equilibrium"). The conceptual origins of homeostasis reach back to Greek ideas regarding the human need to maintain balance, harmony, equilibrium, and the all-round steady-state that was believed in ancient times to contribute fundamentally to good health.

The Greek philosopher Heraclitus (540–480 BC) was ahead of his time when he hypothesized that a static, unchanged state was *not* the natural human condition; rather, he believed, all living things had the intrinsic ability to undergo constant change. A few decades later, his countryman Empedocles (490–430 BC) made the corollary statement that balance or harmony was a necessary condition for the survival of living organisms. Next came a third Greek, Hippocrates (c. 460–c. 377 BC)—called the father of Western medicine—who compared health to harmonious balance, and illness and disease to systemic disharmony.

Then about 150 years ago, French physiologist Claude Bernard (1813–1878) stated in his College de France medical lectures of 1854 that maintaining the internal environment— that which surrounded the body's cells—was essential for sustaining the life of the organism. In 1932, physiologist and medical researcher Walter B. Cannon (1871–1945) extrapolated Bernard's conclusions into his theory of homeostasis, a process of synchronized adjustments in the internal environment that resulted in the maintenance of specific physiological variables within defined parameters—including blood pressure, temperature, pH levels, and others—all with clearly defined "normal" ranges, or *steady-states*.

What all this means is that any threat to our sense of stability (i.e., intensified feeling of stress, weakness, and/ or vulnerability) might originate from the external or internal environment, and could prove physically *or* emotionally distressing.

But here is the most important piece in the homeostasis story: Cannon (who by the way, was chair of the Department of Physiology at Harvard Medical School and president of the American Physiological Society, and coined the term *fight or flight*), emphasized that: "Regardless of the nature of the danger to the maintenance of homeostasis, the response from the body would be the same."

This suggests that although the heat in the room may not go up, if a person's emotional "heat" rises, then his body will react to this stress state and attempt to regain homeostasis quickly by initiating the primitive and impulsive routines to stabilize. The point is, there may not be an actual tiger in the room, threatening to bite off your leg; but those files you're supposed to be working on (the metaphorical tiger in the room) are creeping up on you, threatening to leap at you and eat away at your time resource, so your body will attempt to reestablish homeostasis by lashing out at them as if they were a predator.

Or, that new data entry system may not literally look like a disease bacterium under the microscope, but that does not mean that your body is not going to treat it as one, causing you to take a sick day to recover from the "destabilizing viruses" infecting you in the form of IT initiatives, management meetings, client complaints, new people at work, or adjustments to your usual work schedule.

Day Seven Action

Make a point today to notice how you feel physically. Are you tired (didn't sleep well last night), wired (had too much caffeine this morning), sluggish (from that huge pasta meal you had at lunch), or tense (you were expecting a night of romance and it did not work out)?

Notice how others look to you. Do they appear sickly, lethargic, or sleepy, or perhaps are bouncing off the walls with nervous energy or energy of another sort? What about their mood would you put down to what may be going on inside of them, rather than outside of them?

Manage Primitive Impulses Now
External Examination

One of the best ways to adjust mood is to pay attention to what is happening externally, rather than trying to "think yourself"—or help others "think themselves"—into a better state of mind. If you or those you work with are "down," consider giving them more daylight; this will help them produce more serotonin and, hence, feel better.

Exercise, anything from light walking to power lifting, also will have a positive effect on the neurochemicals dopamine, endorphin, and serotonin. Laughing, too, lowers levels of stress hormones and strengthens the immune system.

Massage is another good way to raise levels of oxytocin; but in the workplace, unless organized in a professional manner, massage can easily give the wrong impression and eventually precipitate a visit to HR for a written warning. Finally, if tempers are flaring and behaviors are getting really aggressive among your colleagues or clients—"in your face," tough to handle, and really "mental" (as in the chapter's opening story)—do as my friend and client, the quite brilliant manager Michael Leckie does when he gets railed on by someone completely out of control: He thinks to himself, "This *can't* be about me." Taking this initial attitude that the more demanding moods and feelings of others are internal to them, and not caused by you, can give you the detachment you need to start to really understand their problems.

Michael rightly says, "I know that whatever is happening is of course either about me, about them, or about us. But in order for me to remain calm enough to be able to truly hear what the issue is, I need to initially depersonalize it." Of course, our primitive brain is self-centered and instinctively wants to make everything, all the time, about us—personal. But this causes us to be defensive and not hear the problem. It may very well turn out to be something we've contributed to; but by starting out with the attitude that "this can't be about me" and having a real desire to help, we can remain calm enough to hear what they're saying and to ask how it could best be fixed for them.

In the end, it's not *all* about you. More about that in Part Two.

Week 11

Relationships
Who Made This Mess?

> *Before you diagnose yourself with depression and low self-esteem, first make sure that you are not, in fact, just surrounded by assholes.*
>
> —William Gibson

I like both country and western music. For someone obsessed with understanding human behavior, nothing drags relationships through the dirt more effectively than country music. It's chock full of cheatin', achy-breaky hearts, gunpowder and lead; and not just in love but at work, as well, whether it's "sticking with it" and dealing with the bossman 9 to 5, or packing bags and walking off down the railroad tracks, sick of work—the boss such a jerk—and not caring about getting fired.

There is an interesting evolutionary theory that proposes there's a benefit to exploring the potential prizes and punishments for our actions by listening to the lyrics of songs like these. Doing so allows us to experience the emotions and outcomes they provoke, but within the safety of our imagination, before we decide whether or not to try them out for real—a bit like this book, but with the added bonus of listening to Dolly Parton or Kenny Chesney.

Given how heated relationships can become, and the primitive impulses they can produce, you can understand how useful it would be to be able to work out some of the problems of your relationships *before* you commit to solving them by "wastin' bullets."

So before you blame your problems at work on your own lying, cheating, cold, dead-beating, two-timing, double-dealing, mean, mistreating heart, read this section, which is designed to help you understand that when the people around you are in a bad mood, it's not all about you.

Everything you have discovered in Week One about the way your primitive instincts can run your life is happening to others, too.

Quite often that blame for shocking behaviors justifiably falls at the feet of those around you. Sometimes the blame is yours. Sometimes the responsibility is shared.

This week's work is all about understanding the primitive nature of our *relationships* and the impulsive behaviors that go with along them. This way you can keep your cool and help others around you do the same.

This way we can all avoid putting Mama in the graveyard, Papa in the pen, and instead, perhaps get some loving done.

Day 8

Relationships Are Dyadic
It Starts with Your Mother!

There were three of us in this marriage, so it was a bit crowded.
— Diana, Princess of Wales

Today you'll tame:

◆ Clinging to the apron strings

Jennifer is trying her very best to manage her client, but the recent churn in the client's team is keeping her from moving ahead with the project. During meetings she tends to direct all her remarks to the lead, with whom she started this project; she avoids developing individual relationships with the other team members. Jennifer is perhaps unconsciously presuming that her relationship with the team leader—the "mother" of this whole project—serves as a proxy for her relationship with the other team members.

(continued)

(continued)

This, of course, is only causing animosity between Jennifer and the new team members, who now seem to be working against her.

"Why can't they just get on board, take my lead, and pull together as a team, for the sake of the project and the business?" she fumes inside.

Can Jennifer develop closer working relationships with *all* the members of a group, and not just the single authority figure, in order to align the whole group around her and the initiative? Will she be able to see past her primitive impulse for latching onto certain individuals and totally detaching herself from others?

We are primitively programmed by our earliest life experiences to form *dyadic relationships*. This means that we tend toward one-to-one connections rather than with groups of people.

Yes, it will sometimes feel like we have a relationship with an entire group; however, that sensation is usually a reflection of the relationships we have with the individuals who comprise the group. These relationships, and our feelings about them, inform our judgment of what the group as a whole means to us, and how we feel about it.

Here's why our relationships really are all one-on-one:

Madonna's First Imprint

For the first nine months of your life, quite probably there was only you and your mother. It was a strong connection between just the two of you.

For most of us, until we began separating from Mom, somewhere between 18 months and 2 years of age, this primary relationship was the only really important one. This, our very first human connection, laid down powerful neural tracks that last a lifetime—and, in a very physical way, imprinted some of the requirements for all our subsequent relationships.

Ducks in a Row

The notion of *imprinting* comes largely from the work of Austrian zoologist and Nobel laureate Konrad Lorenz (1903–1989). He found that when ducklings hatched, they would spend about a day or so looking for a *mother figure*. The ducklings' very primitive brains searched using a single minimum specification to define that figure: it had to move.

If something, anything, moved, the ducklings would follow it. Once the ducklings were imprinted to a creature or object other than their genetic duck mother, and were subsequently returned to their actual mother, they would ignore her completely, choosing instead to follow the individual or object to which they had been initially imprinted.

In one experiment Lorenz imprinted a duckling to a balloon: He simply carried the balloon around and the duckling followed it. Later, as an adult, that same duckling would neither court nor mate with members of its own species. Instead, it would exhibit all its courtship behavior only to round objects. The implication of this experiment is that early imprints upon an organism can influence later life behaviors, some of which are essential to that organism's, and even the species', survival. Lorenz believed that imprints were established at certain critical neurological periods, and that once the critical period had passed, whatever had been imprinted was permanent; it could not be reprogrammed.

The Born Identity

Human beings are similar to other animals in that our early childhood experiences also affect specific aspects of our individual intellectual, emotional, social, sexual, aesthetic, and core beliefs development. Of course, the nature of our imprinting affects our ability to survive and socialize; it also defines some characteristics of our personality and level of self-awareness.

As you might now expect, there is a huge survival advantage to the evolutionary adaptation of imprinting. Behavioral imprinting acts as a survival instinct in newborns, enabling them to immediately recognize their parents and, therefore, maximize their survival in the face of threats that could emerge immediately after birth—such as attack by a predator. Imprinting is very reliable in laying the foundation for forming strong survival-based social bonds between offspring and parents.

So, while we are generally all born with similar reflexes and instincts, some behavioral drivers—including our imprints—are the result of the neural pathways that have been programmed into our brains at various early stages of our development. These are the ones associated with categories such as our family, neighborhood, school, religion, and culture—that is, the components of our environment as a whole.

All life experiences mold our neural connections in some way, which explains their lasting effect on us. These neural connections are crucial in defining, among other things, our values and beliefs; creating our emotional makeup; directing our responses to events and to each other; and ultimately, influencing our desires and goals and highlighting the things about which we are concerned. They will also inform how we communicate all of these. In other words, all of our thoughts, feelings, and actions are both created and constrained by our neural circuitry—which is, in many ways, unique for each of us.

At the most formative stage in our neural development, we are wired with the desire and the need for strong, one-to-one, interpersonal relationships. If we didn't have this desire, we might act in ways which caused our mothers to feel rejected . . . And that would threaten our survival.

Which takes us back to the story at the beginning of this chapter: If Jennifer wants to form relationships with each of the team members, she needs to do the work required to forge those individual relationships. This may mean, for example, creating opportunities to have one-to-one conversations with each of them—lunches, coffee breaks, watercooler encounters, and phone or video calls. Notice I did *not* include e-mail conversations, because, as many of us know, electronic mail lacks the necessary nonverbal signals—eye movement, facial expressions, body language, and voice tone—that our primitive brains use to interpret one another's intentions and inform our decisions about trustworthiness, intention, and friendliness.

Brainwashing

Popular culture is full of ideas and advice about how to alter the innate programming of our minds—whether through self-help or therapeutic psychological processes, quasi-religious organizations, or the dark underworld of an intelligence agency. We are fascinated by the possibility that we might be able, in some way, to undo and reprogram the scripts that have been "written" into our minds.

Is this really possible?

It is true that certain parts of our brain are "plastic"; that is, they have the capacity to change and restructure themselves. And there may be some ways you alone can reprogram your neural networks, as well as some organizations that can help you alter your behavior via neural reprogramming. Certainly, the LSD-fueled CIA MK-Ultra Monarch program for creating Manchurian candidates is documented to have existed (it was

(continued)

(continued)

disbanded in 1973). (Lorenz, the Nobel award-winning psychologist mentioned previously, was in his earlier years the Nazi psychologist who contributed to the earliest ideas about all this.)

But for average Joes and Janes, like you and me, the chances of washing away all our personality traits and starting again, without incurring a whole bunch of pain and risk, and taking off a lot of days from work, are small.

Furthermore, you are probably an "okay person" already. You may just need better ways to manage the tough situations you encounter—not a complete reboot of your system.

As Harvard psychologist Timothy Leary (once described by President Nixon as the most dangerous man in America) said, "You're only as young as the last time you changed your mind."

I Blame The Parents

Realizing that we are all imprinted in some way can help us understand why we, and others, behave as we do—and therefore have the kind of relationships we often do with certain kinds of people.

If your mother is a duck, for instance, it says a lot about you as well. And if your mother is a balloon, you are more likely to be most comfortable hanging around with other balloons, or at least with a balloon's minimum specifications—round, smells like rubber, moves gently, generates static.

On top of all of this, our reptilian brain's self-centered approach to life leads us to mistakenly assume that others think and feel the same way we do; that they have been imprinted in the same way. If, say, I bring you home to meet my mother and you ignore her because to you she is a balloon—well, you can understand how this would cause some friction and "electricity" in the room.

Your definition of "mother" may be different from mine, just as my definition of "work" may be totally alien to you. How we each have been imprinted at key moments in our lives— by our parent figures, siblings, teachers, youth or community leaders, cultural icons, heroes, celebrities, mentors, and bosses, among countless others—will ultimately affect the way we see the world and relate to or disconnect from the others in it.

Day Eight Action

Take notice of all of your one-to-one relationships at work. Which ones are the most satisfying; what do you and the others involved in those relationships do to contribute to that satisfaction?

Notice when there are more than two of you in a group, who speaks to whom, and who gets ignored?

Simply by recognizing that you have the impulse to attach to some people and to ignore others will help you to manage your behavior in groups and around individuals.

Make a point today of connecting with someone you usually pay no attention to in one of your work groups or organization. Make more eye contact with her, chat with her, ask for her input, or invite her for coffee. You may find that you share more of a connection than your primitive brain initially judged in the fraction of a second it took to make its initial decision about this relationship.

As suggested earlier, this would be good advice for Jennifer in the story at the start of this chapter. She needs to connect in some way with each and every member of the team, not just the leader, if she is going to drive her project forward successfully. It will take time, and it may be tough going with some of the members; and, certainly, there is no guarantee of success—all of which the primitive brain is totally averse to. But all relationships require work, to make them work.

Manage Primitive Impulses Now
Appreciation

To our primitive brain, great relationships start with similarity—not only in the way we look to each other but in the way we view and value everything around us. Impulsive conflicts often erupt over a viewpoint a person has that we simply don't share. It is very easy for that person to notice your behavior around this conflicting viewpoint and hence start to regard you as an enemy. Unless you come to some sort of agreement, you are going to be at odds with each other—and sometimes in a very aggressive way.

Now, you obviously won't—nor could you—agree with every person about everything; even if it were possible, it would make life boring. However, it *is* important to become aware that we can acknowledge another person's point of view yet not *agree* with it. For example, it is far better to say "I understand that you have this perspective," rather than "You are wrong." Likewise, saying "I appreciate your concern," or "That is an important point" is a way to acknowledge the person or her intention without saying that her view of the world is the same as yours. Not only will such statements calm your primitive impulses to do battle, they will calm hers, too.

Day 9

Opposites Attract
Missing Out on Great People

You don't have to go looking for love when it's where you come from.

—Werner Erhard

Today you'll tame:

◆ Your compulsive need for another person—like you and your family

Here's a conversation I got into with a colleague, James, over coffee:

James is in his second marriage. It's not perfect, but it is going better than his first.

I asked him about his choice in mates, and he told me that he had fallen in love with his first wife at first sight. They had lots of good times, but lots of bad times, too. He said they wanted different lifestyles, and didn't have much in common. To this he added: "I married my mother—insecure, depressed, dependant on her husband; and she blamed him for the problems in her life."

(continued)

95

(*continued*)

When that marriage ended badly, James decided that he shouldn't trust his impulses when picking a mate. In fact, he believed that anyone he was attracted to would be a repeat of his first choice. He also remembered something that an Asian friend of his had once said: "In the West, your relationships start off hot, and end up cold, whereas in the East—with our arranged marriages—we start off cold, and then warm up."

After taking a year-long break from relationships, James deliberately set about finding a partner to whom he was not necessarily sexually attracted, but who wanted similar things in life and had hobbies and pastimes similar to his. He thought he had found this in Stephanie, and was encouraged that, at first, she also had no initial attraction to him. For a time, she rebuffed all his advances, but gradually they began to form a friendship and, eventually, became lovers. Twenty years later, they are still married and very much "together."

However, James also told me he thinks that this time he married his father—a quiet man who avoids conflict and needs a lot of personal space. I asked him whether he thought he had succeeded in escaping his early imprinting? With an ironic smile, he said, "No, but being married to my father is better than being married to my mother."

Now that's something you don't hear at work too often! However, you do see some of the same patterns of impulsive attraction toward certain types of coworkers happening in workplace, just as you find people drawn time and time again to certain types of partners. In short, we are frequently attracted to people who reflect our dysfunctional past, which feels normal to us but inevitably causes us some pain.

How can we break this cycle and seek to forge relationships that bring us happiness and help us function at our best at work and in our personal lives?

What many of us call "falling in love" is much more likely to be "falling into patterns" of attraction. In our most primitive biology, we tend to follow no one pattern—such as either opposites-attract (diversity) or likes-attract rule (genetic similarity), reproductive potential (ready, willing, and healthy) or even proximity (from the same territory)—we use a combination of *all* of them. Moreover, we look for the complement to many of these aspects of our primitive biology.

You Complete Me

A *complement* is something that makes up the whole. It's the thing that is missing.

> In geometry, complementary angles are angles that are adjacent so that their non-shared sides form a right angle (i.e., 90°).

> In grammar, a complement is the object needed to complete the sentence.

> In human partnerships, a complement is what we innately feel will make up for what we, as individuals, lack.

A complement is also a counterpart, diversity, within a set of "must-have" criteria. In this respect, a complement is not the opposite; nor is it the same. Remember, we are comfortable within only a thin slice of experience, so when we think we have partnered with someone very different from us, perhaps we have, unknowingly, partnered with someone very, very similar.

One problem with connecting with people who fit *our* pattern is that, unfortunately, it causes us to impulsively miss out on some great people!

Attractive

Evolutionary psychologists and biologists have long been interested in factors that lead people to the mates they choose.

One influential study in the 1990s by Swiss zoologist Claus Wedekind at Bern University—dubbed the "T-shirt study"—asked women to describe their attraction to members of the opposite sex by having them smell T-shirts that men had worn. The findings showed that, like many other animals, humans transmit and recognize information pertinent to sexual attraction through, among other signals, chemical substances known as *pheromones* (which the ants I described in Chapter Two used to communicate their path).

Women participating in the study seemed to prefer the scent of men whose immune-system genes were most different from their own. These genes permit a person's body to recognize microorganisms as foreign invaders, and to provide protection from them. From an evolutionary standpoint, scientists believe children are healthier when their parents' immune-system genes vary, because they are protected from more bugs.

Tell Me about Your Mother

The story at the start of this chapter sounds a little Freudian, doesn't it?

Recall that James recognized his pattern that led him to be attracted to women with the behaviors of his mother, which he intuitively accepted (due to his imprinting) from his formative years as befitting those of a "wife"—in this case, insecurity, depression, dependency, and finger-pointing. Is this really the same thing as "falling in love with your mother?"

Science tells us that siblings who are brought up apart from each other may, when they meet as adults, find one another highly sexually attractive. This phenomenon, known as *genetic sexual attraction*, suggests that our genes express behaviors that find their likenesses attractive, and seek out those likenesses to help perpetuate them. But there are serious health risks associated with inbreeding, so evolution has also adapted us away from this natural attraction to our closest genetic likeness. The opposite phenomenon is called *reverse sexual imprinting* (also known as the Westermarck Effect, after the nineteenth-century evolutionary sociobiologist Edvard Westermarck [1862–1939] who first described it formally). The effect occurs when two people, who lived in close domestic proximity during the first few years in the life of one of them, become desensitized to later close sexual attraction for the other.

Sigmund Freud disagreed.

No doubt, because it has become a mainstay of popular psychology over the last century, you have heard about Freud's argument that members of the same family naturally lust after one another, making it necessary for groups to institute taboos around this. Whereas Westermarck argued that such taboos arise *naturally* as products of our instinctual attitudes against such attraction. Many psychologists now believe that Freud's contention that we might be unconsciously sexually attracted to members of our family is incorrect, if not totally absurd.

Perhaps Freud (who was breast-fed by a wet nurse) missed out on the early imprinting and bonding to his mother. He remained adamant that all of us are attracted to members of our families. His belief might be seen as an example of his own primitive best-fit thinking. (Remember this from Chapter Four? Best-fit thinking describes our tendency to try and make square pegs into round ones in order to fit the holes we believe have already been drilled.) So he assumed that everyone had the same imprinting as his. And perhaps he attracted clients like him, too. But he's not here, so we can't ask him. You be the judge.

Where's the Romance Gone?

Some biologists contend that there is a degree of logic to courtship behavior. This evolutionary view of love states that we instinctively select mates who will enhance the survival of the species. Men are often drawn to "classically" beautiful women—those with clear skin, bright eyes, shiny hair, good bone structure, red lips, and rosy cheeks—not because of fad or fashion, but because these qualities indicate youth and good health, signs that a woman is at the peak of her child-bearing years and ready to mate.

This model also suggests that women select mates for slightly different biological reasons. Because youth and physical health aren't essential to the male reproductive role, women instinctively favor men who not only display good genes—such as symmetrical faces—but who also possess pronounced *alpha male* qualities; that is, they have the ability to dominate other males and bring home more than their share of the "kill." The assumption is that male dominance ensures the family group's survival more effectively than youth or beauty. Thus, a 50-year-old chairman of the board—the human equivalent of a silver-backed male gorilla in terms of power over critical resources—is as attractive to women as a young, handsome, virile, but less financially successful male.

Trophies and Gold Diggers

Let's put aside for a moment the indignity of having our attractiveness to the opposite sex reduced to our breeding and food-/income-producing potential. The next time you think that you have met your "soul mate," consider that your deep feelings of attraction might be coming from your reptilian brain—the place from which your strongest instincts originate.

This brings us to another field of study, social psychology, to explore what is known as the *exchange theory* of mate selection. The basic idea here is that we select mates who are more or less our equals. When we are on a search-and-find mission for a partner, we size each other up as coolly as a chartered business valuator assessing a merger, noting our respective physical appeal, financial status, and social rank, as well as various personality traits such as kindness, creativity, and sense of humor. We tally up each other's scores with computer like speed; and if the numbers are roughly equivalent, the trading bell rings and the bidding begins.

The exchange theory gives us a more comprehensive view of mate selection than the simple biological model. It's more than youth, beauty, and social rank that interest us, say some social psychologists; it's the "whole person." For example, this model posits that negative criteria, such as a woman "past her prime," or a man with a low-status job, can be offset by other factors, such as that he or she is a charming, intelligent, compassionate person.

A third hypothesis, known as the *persona theory*, adds another dimension to the phenomenon of romantic attraction. This theory maintains that an important factor in mate selection is the way a potential suitor enhances our self-esteem. According to the theory, each of us has a mask, a *persona,* the face we show to other people, and suggests that we will select a mate who will enhance this self-image. The big question we seek to answer here is: "What will it do to my self-image if I am seen with this person?" We have all experienced pride—and conversely, at times, embarrassment—due to the way we believe that others perceive our mates. Whether we acknowledge it or not, it does indeed matter to us what others think about them. (We'll talk more about this when we look at the importance of the tribe in Week Three.)

You have met thousands of people over your lifetime so far. Let's suppose, as a conservative estimate, that several hundred of them were physically attractive or successful enough to catch your eye. When we narrow this field by applying the social exchange theory, we might come up with a more select group of, say, 50 or a 100 who have a combined "point value" equal to or greater than yours. Logically, then, you should by now have fallen in love with scores of individuals. Yet most of us have been deeply attracted to only a few.

Chances are that the few individuals who truly caught our eye tend to resemble one another quite closely. Take a moment and think about the personality traits of the people you have seriously considered as mates. If you were to make a list of their predominant personality traits, you would probably discover a lot of similarities—including, surprisingly, their negative characteristics.

This tendency supports a simple yet powerful fact: We stay in—and repeatedly gravitate toward—similar relationships, good and bad, both at home and *at work*.

It appears that each one of us is compulsively searching for our complement, both in our personal and work lives, driven by a very particular set of positive and negative personality traits. Scary, perhaps; but less so if you know what those traits are.

See That Really Annoying Person? It's You!

The point is, if you realize that you connect with the same kind of annoying people time and time again at work, it may not actually have anything to do with *them*. It likely has to do with the similarities, the complement, you are naturally seeking.

Ouch. That maybe hit a nerve!

Old-Brain Logic

When it comes to partnerships, the old brain is constantly asking the primeval question: "Is it safe?" And remember, to the primitive brain, *familiar* is safe.

To recap: We're highly selective regarding our choice of mates. More specifically, we appear to be searching for a "one and only," who exhibits a very specific set of positive and negative traits. We are looking for that one person who has the predominant characteristics of the people who raised us. The ultimate reason you fall in love with your "ideal" is not that she is young and beautiful, or that he has an impressive job, or has a "point value" equal to yours, or a kindly disposition. You fall in love because your primitive brain has found a partner whose behavior aligns with and complements (some say "resonates" with) your early neural imprints. He or she is the person your primitive brain has been searching for.

This same resonance with early neural imprints explains why we intuitively connect with certain people we work with and impulsively disconnect with others.

Day Nine Action

Notice what it is that attracts you to people at work. I don't necessarily mean sexual attraction here; more, professional attributes that draw you to work with them, because you feel you'll "get along." How are they similar to you; how are they different? What about them is a complement to you, and vice versa?

Notice how you act around the people at work you feel are *not* part of your complement, as well as how you react to people who are. What are your theories about what attracts others to work with certain people; notice the complements to their behaviors?

Now think about the people at work whose behavior irritates you. To what extent does their annoying behavior complement your own? It may not match your behavior exactly, but it could be similar. You might say it harmonizes with some of your behaviors or "resonates" with them.

Manage Primitive Impulses Now
Point of Attraction

You will inevitably face conflict with the people you have differences with. However, you may also find that you are also drawn to them because certain of their patterns—some positive, others negative—are familiar to you. If you focus on the positive similarities, you'll find any conflict with them easier to manage.

Most likely you will always be drawn to people who resonate with your early upbringing (usually, your biological family). Like James in the story at the start of this chapter, maybe you can think about those attributes of your family members you most like to be around, and then try to find them in people you work with, rather than impulsively gravitating toward them all—including the bad ones.

Day 10

BFFs

One Mind in Two Bodies

The language of friendship is not words but meanings.
                                            —Henry David Thoreau

Today you'll tame:
◆ Some social risks

There is a story of two guys who were introduced to one another at a fete where one of them was playing in the band. Although they were from different parts of the city, there was an instant connection between them. One found the other impressive because he knew all the chords to "Twenty Flight Rock"; the other was amazed by the first's ability to just make up the words to songs.

The two would spend most days sitting opposite each other playing their guitars, trading tunes, rhythms, chords, and lyrics. They became great friends; closer than friends, in fact. They would often say they were "like brothers."

(continued)

(*continued*)

A few years later, they revolutionized the music world and became what many consider the most important song-writing duo ever.

The two men were John Lennon and Paul McCartney.

No doubt you've had one or more best friends (BFFs) over your lifetime. And you may have sometimes wished that your life partner could be like your best friend. You may also occasionally have felt it would be nice to have a best friend at work, since that's where you seem to spend most of your time.

Perhaps you *do* work with your best friend, which is fantastic at times, but even as John and Paul often found, a challenge other times.

My guess is, your best friend just showed up one day, and at some point along the path of the developing relationship, you became best friends. And it's great when you meet your Paul McCartney or John Lennon. But until fate (which, traced back far enough, is perhaps simply biological inevitability) hands you a royal flush of ideal coworkers to spend most of your days with, how are you going to establish more friendly connections with your current colleagues about whom you currently feel only indifferent to?

Me, Again

Best friends share a lot of things—beliefs about the world, interests, behavioral rhythms, likes and dislikes. They have similar values, and support each other's goals. More than likely, your best friend laughs at the same kind of jokes you do. She cries at the same scenes in the movie theater, and understands how you feel without your needing to say anything.

We humans feel good when others understand us. We feel frustrated when they don't. And when we understand each other at an emotional level, we achieve a heightened state of connection—what Thomas Lewis, in his renowned 2000 book, *A General Theory of Love*, refers to as "limbic resonance."

Marching to the Same Drummer

Limbic resonance happens when the neural connections in our limbic system—the part of the primitive brain that only social mammals have—aligns with someone else's. Cats and dogs, horses, elephants, and humans all have limbic systems; snakes and lizards do not. Animals with a limbic system live in groups and raise their young. Those without them—such as reptiles—live solitary lives, and have been known to even eat their young. The only reason that you will find a bunch of snakes hanging out together is because that's where the food is, or the sex.

Mothers and infants have limbic resonance, as do new lovers and best friends. These are all relationships for which we're willing to give up our desire for autonomy and differentiation and enter into a profound neurochemical connection between our respective limbic systems—that part of our brain that governs emotions and relationships. When we do, we are no longer alone.

Trust It

More than likely you find it is easy to work with a person who regards you as a friend, and conversely find it almost impossible to do business with a person who doesn't. That's because we trust our friends more than we do most others, especially in uncertain situations.

Trust in Me

I define "trust" as the ability to predict another person's behavior with reasonable accuracy. Based on experience, I can trust that my friend and colleague Bruce will keep any commitment that he makes to me—for example, to pick me up on time for our visit to a potential client. I can also trust that he won't want to "sell" to that client, preferring to take a more consultative role, which is more comfortable for him, thus giving me the space to lead any "close" on the deal.

Trust deepens for me when I have a sense (again, based on experience) that the other person has my best interests at heart. That means he won't knowingly do anything to harm me. Experience has taught me that anything Bruce might say to me that might sound aggressive or hurtful is not meant that way; it wasn't intentional; it did not mean what it sounded like. I can let it go.

Trust pervades human societies. It is indispensable to maintaining friendships, love, families, and organizations. Trust also plays a key role in economic exchange and politics (if only to the extent that you might not trust politicians as far as you could throw one).

An absence of trust among trading partners often causes market transactions to break down. Without trust in a country's institutions and leaders, political legitimacy falters. Even the best-written contract between business partners is of no value if they do not trust each other. When one partner fails to act in good faith, a contract is of use only for the purpose of litigation. As many of us know, this is a costly venture, one that can take years to complete, and which usually enriches only the lawyers involved and leaves a bitter taste in the litigants' mouths.

Chemical Wedding

The mammalian hormone oxytocin, as explained in Chapter Seven, plays a key role in social attachment and affiliation, and prompts a substantial deepening in trust among humans. Oxytocin receptors are distributed in various brain regions associated with behavior, such as pair bonding, maternal care, sexual behavior, and the ability to form normal social attachments. This chemical permits us to overcome our natural tendency to avoid too-close proximity to others, and thereby facilitates prosocial approach behaviors.

One of oxytocin's many effects is to strengthen an individual's willingness to accept social risks that arise through interpersonal interactions. It does this by inhibiting the activity of the amygdala, the region of our primitive brain involved in instigating fear. Without oxytocin, we wouldn't bond; we would, in short, become socially phobic. An increase in oxytocin helps us trust, and bond with others.

How do we increase oxytocin?

One way is through touch.

As I've said before, nobody needs a sit-down with HR to learn about inappropriate touching. But a warm handshake is safe, and makes a lot of sense, even when you exchange one with those you work with every day. As in other kinds of relationships, we often forget over time how useful it is to make physical contact at work to establish or enforce a solid psychological connection.

Eyes

Our bodies also release oxytocin when we make pleasant eye contact with anyone, even a stranger. Such visual contact does not rely on your knowing the other person; you could make eye contact with someone you pass by as you're walking down the street, or entering or standing in an elevator. Look another person in the eye for a couple of seconds while smiling, and give a nod of subtle acknowledgment.

Choose a Smile

Smile scientists (sounds like a fun job, doesn't it?) have identified over 50 different types of smiles, and research has found the most trustworthy to be the "Duchenne smile," named after the eighteenth-century French neurologist Guillaume Duchenne (1806–1875). He not only deepened our understanding of the conductivity of neural pathways, he also produced the first study on the physiology of emotion, titled *Mécanisme de la Physionomie Humaine (The Mechanism of Human Physiognomy),* a book that subsequently proved seminal to Darwin's later work.

Duchenne was also the first to articulate how the most sincere smiles extend into the eyes via the lower facial muscles, involuntarily causing one to squint. Thus, the trustworthy smile is more than the lips turning up at the corners; it also is reflected in what we call crow's feet. Unless, of course, you've had Botox, in which case you've forfeited the capability to manipulate certain muscles around the eyes. Yes, your skin may look younger, but your smile might look insincere. (There are rewards and penalties for every choice you make!)

Tests suggest that the majority of us are capable of giving, without possessing the corresponding feeling, on demand (in other words what some might call "faking") a crinkly Duchenne smile, as long as we don't rush it; the longer we smile, the more convincing it is likely to be.

Tests have also shown that the majority of us are particularly bad at recognizing insincere smiles. Some scientists believe the reason is that it may be easier for people to get along when they don't always know what others are *really* thinking and feeling.

Believe it or not, giving a stranger a small smile, along with making eye contact as you pass by, can have a huge impact on her feelings *and* her health. Even the briefest eye contact, or a smile, or both, can make people feel connected to others.

Definition of a Friend

I was once offered this definition of "friends": They have a twinkle in their eye when they see you coming, and they have no agenda for your improvement.

I quite like this description. I also am aware that it may, from time to time eliminate some people (who we feel should be our friends) from the category—spouses, parents, bosses, customers, and so on—all of whom may have an agenda for our improvement. Often it's because they have our best interests at heart, but other times it's to satisfy their own self-interests.

Friends with Benefits

Oxytocin has been shown to amplify our ability to remember happy, smiling faces. My guess is that if you flash a smile at someone, she'll associate you with others she regards as happy. It sounds obvious, but smiling really does make *everyone* feel better.

Feel happy, and the concomitant rise in the level of oxytocin relieves the feeling of fear in our reptilian brain by tempering activity in the amygdala—the part of the primitive brain that has some control over fear, anxiety, and defensive behaviors.

Smiling also alleviates the fear you may engender in others around you. So if fear is a major contributor to some of the more impulsive behaviors you witness in yourself and others at work, try flashing a smile at your colleagues a few times a day; you might just find it calms things down. You could also, in the process, make some new friends or even make a connection with people about whom you previously felt indifferent.

Day Ten Action

Notice whom you smile at today, and whom you don't. How do you feel about those you have the impulse to smile at versus those you don't?

Notice whose eyes twinkle when they see you coming. How do you feel about them? Are they also the kind of people who tend to be accepting of you?

Who, if anyone, is your BFF at work? How do you behave around this individual, and how does she behave around you?

Manage Primitive Impulses Now
Go On, Give 'Em a Smile!

Probably you have some coworkers with whom you are not friendly at all, but who are, nevertheless, important to your work. And no doubt they know you don't see them as friends. With that in mind, just for today, try smiling at them—a crinkly-eyed Duchenne smile—when you see them (remember to take your time to do it), and then pay attention to how they react. Does it make the day a little better for you? For them?

A simple piece of advice: Smile more often. The smile is a universal signal for "It's all good," and is a very safe way to signal to the majority of people on our planet that they can feel safe with you.

Having a problem with someone? Smile a little more at her.

Are you under stress? Try smiling a little more, just in general.

Is someone having a problem with you? Give that person a smile and see if she smiles back. Now reassess whether she's really having a problem with you, or not.

Whenever possible, make important connections with people face-to-face. When we connect online, we get a small hit of dopamine, the "seeking" chemical mentioned in Chapter Seven, but not the calming effects and feelings of satisfaction from other chemicals such as oxytocin and serotonin. We may be momentarily energized, but our bodies crave more input in order to have a satisfactory outcome, one that may not be available any other way than through direct human contact (or eating a bar of chocolate.)

Seeking and satisfaction go hand-in-hand—or rather, face-to-face. Hand-to-mouth and you may be taking in more calories than you need.

Day 11

Enemies

The People You Hate

You have enemies? Good. That means you've stood up for something, sometime in your life.

—Winston Churchill

Today you'll tame:

◆ The people at work you JUST CAN'T STAND!

"So, what do you think of Pascal?" inquires the head of marketing after the team interview with him.

I am just about to blurt out, "What an insufferable and talentless #$%-clown!" when I am halted by the group who, as one voice, sings his praises as "far and away the best fit for the job."

Yes, sure, his résumé is great, and he fits in well culturally with the organization. But he rubs me the wrong way. Unfortunately, nobody else here seems to feel that way!

What am I going to do when Pascal gets hired (since that, for sure, is going to happen)? Working with him will be like working in my worst nightmare. He's a total jerk. To make matters worse, he's going to be assigned the desk next to mine. I won't even be able to avoid him!

I can't help myself. I just know it's going to be all-out war with someone who's supposed to be my coworker.

It manifests in many forms: aversion, detestation, disgust, dislike, loathing, repulsion, and revulsion. All these feelings are bound up into what we call *hate*.

Racism, sexism, ageism, and any and all other forms of prejudice are ways we bundle those we hate into neat packages. Why do we instinctively, or traditionally, take a strong dislike to certain people? And when we do, how is it possible to work in harmony with them?

Who Goes There?

The human ability to quickly separate friend from foe is an essential survival strategy; it is, however, this same primitive skill that also forms the basis of hate. Because we know that mistaking an enemy for a friend could have deadly consequences, our primitive mental processes are biased toward doubt, caution, mistrust, and dismissal when we are evaluating others. Remember (as explained in Day Three), whenever we have insufficient data, we default to the negative. Therefore, if we lack vital information, or are confused by data about something, someone, or some group because it falls outside the best-fit category, we will define the entity as "bad," as a potential predator and, ultimately, our enemy.

We face more psychological, as opposed to physical, threats in today's modern work world. Nevertheless, we have the same primitive impulse to "destroy the offender," and it often clicks in no matter what kind of threat we're facing.

Recall what physiologist Walter Cannon said about homeo-stasis and our biological need to remain in a state of equilib-rium: "Regardless of the nature of the danger to [maintaining] homeostasis, the [body's] response would be the same."

Therefore, even if the threat we face is conceptual (as opposed to physical), we will still respond physically—even if only *inside* our bodies. We may feel our heart race, our blood pressure spike, and our muscles tense; we may on occasion display our feelings nonverbally, by screwing up our face in anger, disgust or disdain, getting an angry tone in our voice, and perhaps even making threatening gestures.

A Brief History of Hatred

We often need to assign blame when bad stuff happens. And who do we hold responsible for the negative events in our lives? If we want to affirm our stature, maintain our self-esteem, avoid shame, preserve our pride, and in general keep our neurotransmitter levels high enough to overcome adversity, we do not blame ourselves. No; we blame "them," the "others"—the *enemy*. Furthermore, because the primitive brain can't think beyond the moment, we often blame the person in closest proximity to us.

Since we don't like bad things to happen, and since we believe the enemy causes those bad things to happen, we hate them for it.

Our primitive brain functions in a world of snap-judgment and binary thinking; thus, we quickly make assessments in terms of good versus evil. It matters not that this polarized outlook may be incorrect, as we often learn once we are able to see things through a wider and more detailed lens, because the more rapidly we can make decisions about what or who is at fault, the quicker we can work toward over-coming the threat, thereby maintaining homeostasis. And the stronger the feeling of hate, the more we are compelled to take quick, decisive action to destroy our enemy.

Being "right" about who is at fault in a given situation is not the primary concern of our primitive brain. Its job is to motivate us to do something—*anything*—now! Even if we end up identifying the wrong enemy to attack—or have to make one up—taking action based on a negative bias has proven to be a more effective survival model for most of our evolutionary history. Our primitive brain reasons that it's better to make a mistake than to not take any action at all. And yet throughout our lives, most of us have found that blaming our enemies, especially those we create in the heat of the moment, has made us feel, in the long run, anything from a little stupid to unfair to immoral and inhumane.

Annoying Decisions

The alternative to the impassioned cut and thrust of rapid decision making is, as renowned neurologist Antonio Damasio describes in his book *Descartes' Error: Emotion, Reason, and the Human Brain*, a world where no one makes *any* decisions because of the overwhelming time it takes to consciously crunch the data required to be rational and unbiased, rather than emotional and subjective—"a tiresome cost-benefit analysis, an endless outlining and fruitless comparison of options and possible consequences."

Without emotions—including hate—to push us into making a choice and taking some action, absolutely nothing would get done. Yes, some of our rasher decisions turn out to seem like the narrow-minded bungling of a hot-headed baboon. But the alternative is complete stasis.

Another reason we often hate others is to strengthen our positive relationships. Somehow, hostility toward an "other" solidifies the cohesion of "us," enhancing our loyalty and sense of belonging to one another. In this way, we feel superior. Hostility to "them" intensifies our solidarity.

It's also important to understand that feelings of disgust and contempt help us avoid and distance ourselves from those we don't understand. Hate acts, too, as a defense mechanism against the obnoxious behavior of others. We raise ourselves up by comparing ourselves favorably against the viral and plague-like behavior of our enemy; hence, the edict that when society is breaking down, it is best to find a common enemy, to prevent us from turning on each other.

Kill or Be Killed

When we connect positively to one another, we feel empathetic, compassionate, and cooperative, all strengths of human nature. At the same time, these tender feelings leave us vulnerable to others.

"Hating" gives us permission to "do good" by killing off the evil enemy (in the workplace, in politics, on the sports field, in the blogosphere) and still see ourselves as good people. The feared other—the enemy—seems dangerous, and we feel compelled to escape the threat or destroy it. Feeling threatened strongly arouses our simple and primitive urge to "kill or be killed." If you have any doubts about this, pay attention to all the words and phrases used in the business world that have warlike connotations (e.g., "the market is killing us," "we crushed the competition") and even more primitive, territorially aggressive language such as, "We need to throw all the fire power we can at this project and destroy the other side."

It's the Feeling, Not the Situation

There are some situations at work I really *hate*, from the bottom of my heart. Looking at them closely, I realize they make me feel extremely stressed out and often a bit overwhelmed. That's why I hate them.

Ask any person who says he hates his job to give you more details as to why and you will soon find that what he hates are the emotions he experiences on the job, more than the job itself.

There is, unfortunately, no fix for the feelings of hate that some people at work might provoke in us now and again (or, for some, on a minute-by-minute basis). What we can do, however, is to learn to recognize when it is not the people themselves, but the way we feel around their behavior that causes us pain. Doing so focuses us away for a few moments from our primitive impulse toward them, allowing us to think in a more rational way so that we can change our environment (with them in it) to hopefully stimulate more positive feelings within us.

Why Can't They Be Like Us?

We all exist between dichotomies: Some of us like hot chili; others prefer mild. Some pump up their music loud; and others prefer it to play soft in the background. Some seek constant change, while others avoid it at all costs. Yet if theories on homeostasis are true, we are *all* seeking stability. Therefore, the hot chili that causes indigestion for one coworker is pure pleasure for another. The loud music that irritates some colleagues energizes others. Likewise, the constant change motivated by the CEO's "shiny objects syndrome" feels like steady progress to him even though it is disorienting for his staff. We all prefer to approach life from within our own comfort zone;

but it is helpful to recognize that what feels good to us may be *way* outside the comfort zone of others.

Extremists

No doubt, your enemies come across as individuals at the opposite end of some continuum from you—which of course makes it hard to walk the same path with them.

While you are strolling along enjoying the view, they are striding way out ahead, scaring off the wildlife. You prefer to take a structured approach to problem solving; they like to think way outside the box, and drive you crazy with their scattered method of project management. You believe in keeping everything out in the open; they prefer to have private conversations and keep things to themselves, unless you ask. You keep a tidy desk; theirs looks like a landfill site. You think it's best to show your emotions privately; theirs leak all over the place, and often in a way that causes you to worry about how it might affect others. To you they are self-centered, whereas you try to keep everyone's interests top of mind.

Extremities

As the old sound bite goes, we can choose our friends, but we can't choose the family we were born into. Friends of the family are a tricky group, as well; they can be the cause of heated argument when you attempt to avoid hanging out with your mom and dad, or your husband's or wife's cronies for the weekend.

Similarly, while we can decide where to work (well, most of the time), we usually don't get to choose our coworkers, peers, or managers—unless we're the boss, and sometimes not even then. That means we end up spending a great deal of time with people who can be difficult for us to have relationships with—that is, people who we feel to be different from us.

Yet the person who upsets *you* won't necessarily be a problem for *me*, and vice versa. This indicates something very important: *It isn't about them*; it is about you *and* them. The kicker here is that **diversity makes for a stronger team**.

In the same way that genetic diversity makes for healthier people all around, having a diversity of personalities and abilities in the workplace has been shown to improve a team's chances of success. That is why high-performing teams seek and embrace diversity in skills, experience, and thinking. That said, it is important for teams to have similar values and goals. Big problems can arise when these don't align, not only when team members aren't all "sailing toward the same destination," but when the "set of their sail" is radically different, too; because then, regardless of the way the wind is blowing, the team will not all end up in the same place. If there is no foreseeable way to overcome these types of disconnects, we tend to feel powerless, causing the primitive brain's dopamine levels to dip and thus provoke the flight response.

At some point, however, our primitive brain may realize for other important resource reasons it cannot leave the environment—for example, "I'm the boss here," or "I need the job," or "This is stable gig." Such reasons compel it to become aggressive about the differences and battle through them, propelled forward by its fight response.

People Hate Being Powerless

People may hate their bosses because they can't influence or fire them. People hate their jobs when they have no alternative. People also hate problems against which they can't defend themselves.

Let's say that you discover a colleague hates you, or you hate him. It is worth looking into what choices may be available to either or both of you in terms of resolving your differences. In other words, ask yourself: Does this situation render either or both of us helpless and powerless in dealing with each other?

To illustrate, imagine you loathe your coworker, Tom, because he eats very smelly food for lunch every day at his workstation, which is right next to yours. You, on the other hand, work the late-morning to early-afternoon shift because you have to take your kids to school in the morning and pick them up at the end of their day; so you don't get a lunch-time. You are, for all intents and purposes, trapped by your coworker's eating habits, which seems unfair because all you are trying to do is get on with your job to earn a living and support those children. What choice do you have but to grit your teeth and bear it? You don't want to make a fuss and become known as a complainer. You want to stay on this shift; it suits your lifestyle, enabling you to spend more time with your kids. The penalty you pay for that, however, is that between 12:30 and 1:00 PM every day, you get sick to your stomach when Tom eats his lamb samosa three feet from you!

Now as for Tom, he is saving to put down a deposit on a house so he can give *his* kids the kind of environment he believes is necessary for their health and happiness. That's the reason he eats lunch at his desk every day, slaving away and never even taking a half-hour break: He's keeping his eye on the prize while sucking up his own form of punishment. For all you know, maybe he'd love to be able to come in late and leave early every day, like you do. But the cost of housing has risen to a point where he and his wife risk being pushed out of the market if they don't make the bucks they need, fast. Tom can no more ignore the economy than you can ignore your kids if you both are to have the life each desires.

Day Eleven Action

Who at work do you hate? What is it about them that offends you? Do you truly hate them? Or is it more the feeling you get when you're around them that you hate?

Who do others seem to hate, or at least dislike? If you don't feel the same way, what about them is different from you?

Manage Primitive Impulses Now
Take It Offline

Stress and fear can lead us to revert to polarized thinking (right versus wrong, good versus bad, etc.). Fortunately, an unbiased consideration of the evidence, correct thinking, thoughtful dialogue, and empathy can help us overcome these primitive urges to hate. But first we need to alleviate the stress and fear, to give our neocortex the time, space, and energy to do all of the above. Every kindergarten teacher knows the value of a "timeout."

If hate is an issue for you or someone around you, take a timeout. Confronting the anger and fear at the moment it occurs can often lead to further aggression and an escalation of the feeling or of the problems that feeling is causing.

Remember, it is the *feeling* that is produced around that person that you think and say you hate. Concentrate on the feeling, and the behavior it is producing, rather than the person. Once you can identify and describe the behavior and the feeling that goes along with it, consider whether it would be possible to communicate to the person what it is he does that makes you feel the way you do; and evaluate the perceived penalty of taking the risk to bring it up. Maybe you hate someone at work because he is intrusive. When he asks you personal questions, you feel uneasy. The next time this person approaches, and asks, for example, "Did you get any last night?" tell him, "I feel uneasy being asked questions like that."

(continued)

(*continued*)

Of course in doing so, you run the social risk of being left out of the conversation. But at least you have been clear about how you are affected by this behavior and so maybe he won't ask that kind of question again

Can your response to people you find troublesome change their behavior? Maybe not; but it may be worth a try.

Finally, you may need to convince your reptilian brain that, most of the time, for most of us in this modern work world, we have no enemies in the most extreme sense of the word. There are just people who think, feel, and act differently from us.

Day 12

Indifference

You're Not Even on My Radar

Meh.

—Lisa Simpson

Today you'll tame:
◆ Habitual apathy

Michael's business partner approached him at the business networking event and asked exuberantly, "Hey, did you meet Aamaal over there? She is a perfect ally for our business." He then launched into a full description of how well she would fit in.

Michael had, in fact, met her. He just hadn't "clicked" with her. He did, however, fully understand the connection his partner had made with her—but only on an intellectual level. So before the meeting ended, he went over and spoke to Aamaal again. He spent an appropriate amount of time with her before asking for her business card and telling her, "I'll call you."

(continued)

(*continued*)

A day went by, then a week, and still he did not call Aamaal. Another week later, still no e-mail or call to follow up with her and cement their connection. Michael had no strong image when he pictured Aamaal in his mind; no strong feeling about her at all.

Yes, he knew she would make for a great strategic ally; yet he felt totally indifferent to her as a person. He was much more concerned about pursuing a couple of people from the meeting he seemed to get along with, even though they were less than ideal fits for the business. In fact, one was a competitor, but very friendly.

If only Michael were able to push past his primitive brain's personal feeling of indifference toward a potentially great business ally, he might be able to grow his business instead of hanging out and getting pally-wally with the competition.

Have you ever noticed when you go to a conference or networking event, that you won't notice most of the people in attendance? Some may seem friendly to you, others may irritate you, and a few you might want to go home with, but the vast majority of those present will not end up "on your radar," even if they are standing shoulder-to-shoulder with you.

In my case, there is a whole world in which I never get involved; probably that's true for you, too. It's because we do not have particularly strong feelings one way or another for the people in it.

We can understand, intellectually, the potential benefit of forming relationships with many of the people out there; our primitive brain, however, cannot. It is much more involved in making decisions about relationships than we give it credit for. It decides who we team up with and who we could not care less about. Those who don't register as friends, enemies, or potential mates, the primitive brain decides they simply aren't worth our time.

A friend of mine tells the story of how two of his biggest clients came from people his primitive brain was totally indifferent to. How did he win over these two clients? By overcoming his complete indifference to them and treating them as friends. This is why I always see the value of agreeing to coffee dates—no matter who asks, or how I feel about them.

Who?

Consider the research that's been done on human attraction. As discussed earlier on in this book, men can be attracted within a few fractions of a second to women who have healthy skin, and women to men who have symmetrical faces.

Likewise, most managers make the majority of their intuitive decisions about whether or not to hire a candidate within the first few seconds of meeting the person. Such choices can—and often are—biased toward good-looking people, in keeping with what is known as the "what is beautiful is good" stereotype. That means the decision is made before the candidate has even been offered a chair to sit in, and long before the hiring manager asks her neocortex (intelligent or conceptual) questions—and the candidate gives his or her best neocortex answers.

This is not to say that the unattractive *don't* get hired; simply that the attractive benefit from what is called a "halo effect," which draws us to them. As unfair as it may seem, our decisions about how good individuals might be as employees are primed by our unconscious judgments about their attractiveness. To this end, it has been found that beautiful people tend to get better grades, are hired more often, and are paid better than less attractive people.

Both parties in these interactions are influenced by what their primitive brain is looking for when judging a potential new hire, as friend, enemy, potential sexual partner, or "send in the next candidate, please."

Needless to say, this impulsive bias to gravitate toward what the primitive brain deems as "good genetics" discounts our modern world's need, and the modern brain's ability, to appreciate the value of diversity.

Indifference Comes at a Price

Moneyball, the biographical sports film written by Steven Zaillian and Aaron Sorkin (and nominated for six Academy Awards), features a character named Peter Brand, a Yale economics grad (played by Jonah Hill). In a defining moment in the film, Brand says: "People are overlooked for a variety of biased reasons and perceived flaws. Age, appearance, personality . . . Mathematics cut straight through that; . . . of the 20,000 notable players for us to consider, I believe that there is a championship team of 25 people that we can afford, because everyone else in baseball undervalues them." This model for choosing players based on stats, and not bias, in 2004 led, in part, to the Boston Red Sox winning their first World Series title since 1918.

Blending into the Background

Those individuals you do not instantly identify as a friend, enemy, or sexual partner will be filed in your mental wastepaper basket of indifference. This doesn't mean that you do not engage at all with them; rather that whatever you might be doing with them now is merely a surface transaction, not something deep-seated in a primal need. Even if your organization needs these people, your primitive brain may not see them as beneficial to you; you might therefore ignore them or not even be aware they are there. And, yes, they will sense this.

You may find that there are people at work with whom you simply have no meaningful engagement. You may also find that there are some with whom you really need or want to engage but who have no space, time, or regard for *you*. Their primitive brain has decided that you present neither a benefit nor a threat to them. While this can be annoying to you, or them, the biggest loss is to the company. After all, your organization needs you to collaborate, share ideas, update one another, offer support, and so on.

We all know about indifference—in particular, other people's indifference to us—at an instinctive level. Perhaps you've noticed that much of today's consumer-driven markets are geared to overcoming this indifference. Think about makeup, jewelry, fashion, expensive cars, monster homes, the latest iPhone or tablet, or that trendy bar or café. None of these are necessary for our survival, or even our essential well-being, but we spend money on them anyway. What they all have in common is that they improve our chances of being noticed; they *elevate our status*.

And if there is one thing to which we are *not* indifferent, it is our status.

Day Twelve Action

Today, notice the people about whom you feel completely indifferent. Also notice whether others *do* pay attention to that person. What are they noticing, or valuing, that you fail to relate to?

Notice as well those who are completely indifferent to you, as well as those who do show up on their radar.

What do they value that you don't; or what might you be failing to project clearly enough to them?

If you want to get on another person's radar, to be noticed, then be more explicit in projecting values similar to their own. (Examine what you believe to be some of their most positive behaviors and project them back to them.) And if you want to connect with people your primitive brain is telling you are of no value to you, but your business mind says could be helpful, then smile at them, make a coffee date, sit down with them and ask for their opinions on a work issue you both share. See if a more intimate and structured environment causes you to fundamentally reassess how you relate to them.

Executive Indifference

In early 1962, four young Liverpool musicians travelled down to London to audition for Decca Records. They were rejected by an exec at Decca who said guitar music was on the way out. These words would soon come back to haunt the exec when the group, who happened to be called The Beatles, became the most popular and biggest-selling band in the world, turning over half a billion units within 10 years.

Maybe this exec should have taken a second listen to the boys, or asked his colleagues for their view?

Manage Primitive Impulses Now
Off Message

Just as with friends, enemies, and sexual partners, what makes me indifferent to someone may stimulate your interest or even provoke your outrage. It could be something small that someone does or says that tunes me out but has the opposite effect on you.

Never underestimate the power of a single comment or action. What may not stimulate one person can just as easily provoke others. So if you find someone suddenly turns off to you, ask, "Is any of this relevant to you?" Only by asking can you find out what may have caused them to drop out of the conversation or relationship.

Day 13

Moods Are Contagious
Managing Your Mirror Neurology

> *If you need rapport—which I don't think is necessary, most of the time—you could establish it by matching behaviors.*
> —Richard Bandler

Today you'll tame:

◆ The infectious effect of emotions

Taylor, who usually approached meetings with an upbeat, positive attitude, was prepared to lead her first meeting with her new, multinational client as consultant on innovation. She knew she had her work cut out for her; she was aware that innovation is a tricky subject, as it can seem like a bit of a threat to people—even in the most forward-looking organizations.

Unfortunately, the meeting bombed. Those in attendance got the message *intellectually*, but no one showed any enthusiasm for the journey of discovery upon which the company was about to embark. For Taylor, the response was something of a shock, as it was out of the ordinary for one of her presentations.

As a bit of background, Taylor was feeling a bit down that day. The friend she carpools with had just had a death in the family, and although they had not talked about it on the way to work, the mood in the car had affected her.

To counter the sad mood, she could have made a quick call to an upbeat colleague or friend before the meeting to put her in the right frame of mind; but Taylor had not been aware at the time of how people inevitably absorb one another's moods, and how this can then impact the atmosphere at work.

We all know that the common cold is contagious; most of us catch one or more every year. We all also know that washing our hands often during the day, for at least 15 seconds, is the best preventative measure against this virus, which accounts for a massive percentage of the time people take off from work, and costs billions a year in lost productivity. But how can we stave off the black moods of other's, given that they can make our time at work an unproductive misery?

Outbreak

How many times have you been sitting beside someone in a meeting who yawned, and within seconds you yawn, too? You didn't think you were tired. And you aren't! Or, have you ever been working away contently when someone walks by your cubicle nibbling a chocolate bar and suddenly you crave a sweet, too—even though you just had lunch a half hour ago?

Well, moods are contagious, too. We've all experienced having a great day when, at work or at home, someone shows up in a bad mood, and soon we are in a bad mood, too. All of us can "catch" another person's negativity; fortunately, we also can catch a positive outlook just as easily. This tendency, as you can imagine, can be good and/or bad for business, for without question, mood affects our productivity.

Sharing the Feeling

You've very likely been in a situation like this before: You're at work, doing your job, and someone hurries over to tell you something very important, and he seems extremely excited. If he conveys good news to you about something or someone in which you are also interested, or just shares a funny anecdote with you, your mood will undoubtedly improve—at least for a few minutes. Conversely, imagine that a colleague who is clearly angry stops by your office to share with you a perceived injustice perpetrated by senior management . . . well, good luck not getting sucked into that same emotional state.

What if you talk only briefly with someone you don't even know on the street, and immediately notice that his expression is distressed or unhappy? Do you usually find that you are likely to mimic the person's expression—if only for a fraction of a second? Some of us are more likely to pass on our moods to others, due to our more frequent or bolder displays of dramatic facial expressions, and some of us are more susceptible to contagious moods. In psychoanalytic terms, our ego boundary is more *porous*.

Like all of your other primitive brain reactions, emotional contagion happens within milliseconds. It happens so quickly you have no control over it; and because your conscious mind rarely pays attention to this phenomenon, you're not even aware you're being "infected."

The good news is that we are much more likely to be influenced by the more mundane emotions such as cheerfulness, irritability, or melancholy, than by more extreme emotions such as exhilaration, rage, or euphoria. In other words, you're probably not going to flip out just because you witness someone else throwing a tantrum. On the other hand, it *is* pretty easy to absorb a dull mood.

We "catch" certain moods from other people, depending on three factors: (1) the relative strength of the person's mood, compared to that of another; (2) the level of resonance/connection shared by the two people's primitive, limbic brains; and (3) our innate sense of confidence in our own mood.

Emotional Time and Space

Besides being influenced by other people's moods and emotions, we may also unconsciously seek out others who are in the same mood. Often we seek to confirm whatever view they themselves are holding—even if it is a negative one at that moment. In this way, we validate our own outlook by being drawn to others who share it, or by influencing them to catch it. That's why we generally hang around others who feel as we do and help to create an atmosphere that reflects our collective mood. This is great when we are all feeling positive, but potentially limiting when we are not.

Furthermore, our moods tend to focus only on whatever our outlook is *right now*. At the same time, we like to make solid predictions about the future, leading us to formulate theories that we will feel in the future as we do right now—that is, that things will not change. Therefore, we can be happy, and spread happiness, and be optimistic and imagine an optimistic future for ourselves. Or we can take a negative approach, feel pessimistic, and cause those around us to feel pessimistic, too.

We are rarely aware of subtle mood swings taking place within us. Psychologists point out that people are largely unaware that a good or bad mood can produce an optimistic or pessimistic outlook; to us, it simply seems that the facts *support* our view.

Mirror Site

I really like the story of how mirror neurons were discovered, because it involves monkeys and ice cream—a great combination.

In the 1980s and 1990s, Italian neurophysiologist Giacomo Rizzolatti was working with fellow scientists Giuseppe Di Pellegrino, Luciano Fadiga, Leonardo Fogassi, and Vittorio Gallese at the University of Parma, Italy. (Word of warning: Some of you probably won't agree with their research methods.) In their experiments, these researchers placed electrodes in the ventral premotor cortex of macaque monkeys to study neurons specialized for controlling hand and mouth actions—for example, taking hold of an object and manipulating it.

During each experiment, as a monkey reached for pieces of food, the researchers recorded the reaction from a single neuron in the monkey's brain to measure its response to certain movements.

Then one of the scientists took a break from the lab and came back with an ice cream cone. He noticed that the same neurons from which he and his colleagues had recorded data responded when a monkey just *witnessed* him bringing his ice cream cone up to his mouth to eat; it was as if the monkey were eating the ice cream himself.

The article detailing this discovery was rejected by *Nature* magazine for its "lack of general interest." (Maybe they were not big ice cream eaters?) A few years later, however, the same group published a paper reporting the presence of what they called "mirror neurons." A subsequent study, conducted by Ferrari Pier Francesco and his colleagues, described the observation of these mirror neurons responding to facial gestures.

Today, reports on mirror neurons have been widely published, and confirmed with evidence from functional neuroimaging, strongly suggesting that humans have mirror neuron systems. Researchers have identified brain regions that respond during both taking an action and observing an action.

In other words, we humans need only to *see* someone else performing an action to register or *feel* as if we're performing it ourselves.

Emotion, Mirrors, and Empathy

Emotional contagion stems from our primitive ability to mirror the feelings of others and thus empathize with them.

Most people are confident they can interpret the emotions of others from subtle facial expressions, as well as more obvious physical behaviors (what many call *body language*). This process of "reading" another's emotions is mediated by the cells in our brain—the aforementioned mirror neurons—that cause the stimulation of the muscular activities underlying these emotion-based behaviors.

For example, have you ever noticed that if you "act out" the facial expressions or physical gestures and movements associated with an emotional state (like fear, sadness, joy, etc.), you start to actually *feel* something of the emotion itself—and sometimes get quite overwhelmed with the feeling? Indeed, many professional actors use this "method of physical action" to access a real—or as some might refer to it, "authentic"—emotional state so that they can convincingly portray the character they are playing.

Of course, when you watch an actor's performance on film, you know that the emotions he was "feeling" stopped when the director yelled "Cut!" Nevertheless, your understanding of the character's mental and emotional state—which is based on your mirroring of his physical state—creates an emotion in you that you project back onto the character (or monster, or animation, for that matter) on the screen. In other words, the character's emotions feel real to you—and they are, because they are now *your* emotions. You have become empathetic.

We can think of *empathy* as the ability to experience another person's reality. *Mirroring* is the neural mechanism by which we automatically understand other people's actions, intentions, and emotions. Based on this theory, the relatively recent discovery of mirror neurons (c. 1980) is considered by some to be an important piece of the puzzle showing how we connect with others—and, therefore, why we are social creatures. For communication to succeed, however, both the individual sending a message and the individual receiving it must recognize the significance of the signal being sent.

Mirror neurons provide a mechanism for sharing both the feeling and intention of the message—things that often aren't encoded in the message itself. Hence, when we are bonded to our friends, we are able to pick up their meaning better than we can from people we barely know. This is why, when we find it hard to bond or link with someone, we often say we "just don't get them." We might find them confusing; or we may just be indifferent to them.

Sociopathic?

When we interact with people who find it hard to express their feelings, we tend to perceive them as cold or inhuman; indeed, we might easily regard them as threatening.

As I've stated before, we humans are relational beings. We do not function optimally unless we're around others who share our feelings in some way. As poet John Donne wrote, "No man is an island." We prefer to be in a state that is adjoined to a very similar state. If that neighboring state cannot mimic ours, or vice versa, then we are deeply troubled because that is what we are unconsciously designed to do. We all have a deep need to be understood; when we talk to someone, and he doesn't "get" our meaning, or understand the importance of what we are going through, we tend to get frustrated (to say the least). In more extreme cases, we may begin to question the value of the relationship, or even turn the listener into our enemy.

Day Thirteen Action

Notice the effect other people's moods are having on you today. Are they causing a shift in your mood, for the better or worse? Are they provoking some emotions in you? Who is influencing you today?

Who might you be influencing with your mood today?

Manage Primitive Impulses Now
Hazmat Suit

Can we manage our limbic-social brain's impulse to mirror other people's bad moods—say, by staying away from depressed people? Well, probably that's not possible, mainly because you'd eventually run out of people, including yourself, since almost everyone gets down now and again—even the most optimistic among us.

Try this instead: When you are confronted with someone who is in a decidedly bad or depressed mood, remind yourself that you are in a *good* mood, and try not to "catch" the other person's mood. Keep in mind, you are an autonomous human being, that there is "you" and there is "them." So ask yourself, who is going to be

(continued)

(continued)

the boss of you? Why not decide, "Me! I'm the boss of me," and then pick the mood you want to be in, while allowing others to choose their own. Or maybe yours will be strong enough to "infect" them—hopefully in a good way. Do your best to transfer some of your good feelings to other people.

And good luck with that; some bad moods are really tenacious.

Day 14

The Four Stages of Relationship
From Captivate to Cooperate

The hottest love has the coldest end.

—Socrates

Today you'll tame:
◆ The natural cycle of friendship at work

The two of you started out so well.

The interview was fantastic. You both had the same views on the industry and where the company needed to go.

The first six months were a dream. The new hire was giving you exactly what you needed, exactly when you needed it. It was as if she intuitively understood everything that needed to be done.

Yet slowly but surely, the honeymoon period came to an end, and this individual morphed into yet another one of your disengaged employees: she became standoffish, belligerent, and sometimes aggressively argumentative.

(continued)

(*continued*)

Now you have the feeling that either she has "flipped her lid" or is purposely working against you—she is either "mad" or "bad."

Whatever the case, you know one thing: You're going to have to let her go!

When you first met, it was dynamite, but now it is as if she is pouring cold water onto everything, and a new type of spark is flying.

Inevitably, relationships change. Sometimes for the better, but just as often for the worse. As in the rest of life, whether at work or at home, family members, best friends, partners, and coworkers, over time, often "come to blows." What happens after the fallout? How do you continue to work with someone you really hit it off with from day one but have since cooled to, so much that an icy indifference now exists between you; or it has gone the opposite direction, heating up to a deep hatred or intense loathing?

Reflection

When we first meet another person, we either click or we don't—and it can take just milliseconds for us to decide!

"Clicking" means that we have begun to "mirror" the other; failing to click likely indicates that mirroring is not happening. Either way, we get a gut feeling that the person is either a "fit" for us, or not; and that person gets that same primitive impulse about us.

The stages of any intense relationship are the same whether at work or in our personal lives. They are:

1. Infatuation
2. Reality

3. Grief
4. Partnership

Infatuation

The gleam of infatuation we experience at the start of a new relationship is largely the product of potent brain chemistry. And the primary ingredient in that neurochemical brew is dopamine, which we discussed in Day Seven, a neurotransmitter best known for its capacity to initiate muscle movement and pleasure-seeking behavior, as well as its addictive hold over our motivation and moods. It triggers the joyously obsessive nature of first love in the same way it triggers the high of meeting a colleague who sees the picture the same way you do.

We get a sense of euphoria when we find people we really enjoy working with—perhaps along with sleeplessness, loss of appetite, and a rush of energy. Essentially, we experience some of the same sensations when we work with people we like as when we fall in love.

Other people won't necessarily understand why the two of you get on so well, or how it is you can be so productive together. Nevertheless, there's no denying there are fireworks—in a good way—when you work together on projects. The business itself benefits, exploding with productivity, innovation, and a passion for achieving its goals.

For a time.

As cited previously, whether in the workplace or personal life, the infatuation stage with another person is the same. You love having the new person in your life, think they will work out great, and overlook or deny their faults—initially, at least. Simply, you love the feeling that you get when you are around them.

The two of you spontaneously mirror each other. They show up on time, anticipate your moods and desires, and unconsciously adjusts their pace to match yours. And you do the same for them. Life is easy—even delightful. As University of California at San Francisco psychiatry professors Thomas Lewis, Fari Amini, and Richard Lannon explain in their work, *A General Theory of Love,* (and as we explored on Day 10) our nervous systems are not self-contained; rather, "mammals developed a capacity we call 'limbic resonance'—a symphony of mutual exchange and internal adaptation whereby two mammals become attuned to each other's inner states."

Workplace Affairs

I recently came across some stats that said we spend 164 more hours at work per year nowadays than we did 20 years ago. One in three of us eat lunch in our workspace every day, and a third of us don't use up all our vacation days. Do these figures sound about right to you?

Given the fact that we spend so much of our lives at work, it is inevitable that many of us find our sexual partners there—and potentially our life partners (I know I did).

There are, however, some pitfalls for our primitive brain and behavior when we start to "fall for" someone at work. What do we need to look out for when the impulse for lust and/or love hits us?

One thing to keep in mind is that the equal nature of a love relationship may not match the inherent inequality of the workplace hierarchy. Problems often arise when one person in the love relationship works for the other—either directly or indirectly. The way you treat each other outside the office may be very different from the way you have to act at work. This could confuse your primitive brain and make it feel unfairly treated—even angry sometimes.

More tricky is the way you value physical intimacy in your relationship outside of work, which probably will not jive with the way your workplace proscribes physical intimacy between coworkers. And the way you talk to your significant other at work may make some of your colleagues uncomfortable.

Some organizations are dead-set against romantic relationships in the workplace, and institute policies that clearly state that position. They do this for a number of reasons: concerns over abuse of power, security risks, or low productivity, among others.

Of course, given the time coworkers spend together, relationships of a sexual or otherwise intimate nature inevitably form. Some companies put systems in place to address this inevitability. Employees may be allowed to keep working for the group (in another department or branch) and so maintain the romantic relationship they need with their former close colleague.

Who knows? It may be that if the spark ignites for you at your place of work, you may have to pay a visit to HR to seek guidance, come clean, or be led out of the building by security.

Reality

Sooner or later, reality is going to bite and bring you and your colleague at work who are "infatuated" with each other crashing down to earth.

As you spend more and more time together over the months, the mirroring becomes unsustainable. You can walk at the other's pace, laugh at their jokes, and eat when they want to eat, for a few hours, days, or even weeks. Eventually, however, no matter how similar you are and how good your friendship, you will begin to slip back into your own rhythms, moods, and eccentricities, and so will they. You begin to "fall out" of your former limbic resonance. At some point the dopamine, oxytocin, and serotonin rush is going to slow down, and will fail to satisfy, until both of you go "cold turkey."

This could happen over a long period of time or be the result of a single, sudden event. Whatever the case, you either gradually or suddenly realize, perhaps unconsciously, that in some or many respects you are not able to fully share the same views and behave in the same way in certain situations.

You begin to look at each other with some dissatisfaction as you measure this newfound dismay against the fading intensity. But because you are probably tied to the relationship in a number of ways, you can't necessarily "take flight" (in other words, back out of the relationship). It seems to you then that the only way forward is to try to change the other person. This change seems necessary, to relieve the frustration and disappointment you feel because your partner or workmate is no longer behaving the same as you. More importantly, perhaps, you miss the feeling you experienced when the two of you were so delightfully in sync.

This period in a relationship is full of discord. It might start with a slight retreat from one another; but, inevitably, it progresses toward anger—and often aggression—as both of you attempt to change the other person's behavior to mirror your own. Problems between you begin to escalate and intensify as both of you concentrate more and more on what each feels the other is missing, or not doing "right."

You no longer delight in meeting together at work, and become frustrated by, for example, the other's approach to a project; you come to realize you have different ideas, work styles, goals—and most problematic of all, values.

Grief

Then one day you wake up and realize that the other person is not at all who you thought they were. In fact, there are many things about them that annoy you; you might discover you don't even *like* them anymore. Consciously or not, a breakup begins, and along with it, the sense of loss of a great partnership.

You grieve the loss of the person you *imagined* the other to be; you also grieve for the great feelings you experienced at the beginning of the relationship.

Then, however, you find yourself spending time thinking about how to leave the partnership—or even the organization where you both work. You begin to focus on every little annoyance, to confirm your belief that you are working with the wrong person. Professional "infidelity" begins to occur, as you spend time surfing job sites and e-mailing head hunters. The betrayal is complete when one of you quits your job to go work for a competitor.

Workplace Affairs—the Saga Continues

If a breakup happens, you'll find it hard to let go, no matter how painful it is to stay, because you and your friend/partner used to mirror each other in so many ways.

You'll find yourself bumping into each other a lot at work—again, because you used to mirror each other in so many ways. If one of you leaves to take another job, you'll become insanely jealous of the people she now works with; you'll follow her progress on LinkedIn or Facebook. Colleagues will tell you to "get over it," which you will find difficult to take. If you both stay at

(continued)

(*continued*)

the same company, to eradicate thoughts of her, you'll institute a kind of "scorched earth" policy, refusing to work with or near her, which might be hard to do. Regardless, you'll be bereft; a terrible feeling—and all because you used to mirror each other in so many ways.

Always remember, however, that time (or corporate relocation) is the great healer of this grief.

Partnership

The alternative to this painful process is to decide to stay in the relationship and accept the person as they truly are. To do this, you make a commitment to create a partnership based on enjoyment of the positive aspects of alignment you share, and on better managing the areas where you are not so closely aligned.

In order to move forward successfully, it's imperative to do a few things. One is to recognize when differences between you are most likely to occur, and that in the face of these differences you will both need to cope or compromise in order to continue to benefit from your relationship.

Keep in mind that the best-performing teams are typically made up of people who have differences—different educational and training backgrounds, different cultural backgrounds, different ideas, different approaches. In spite of their differences, however, these high-performing teams share two important things: values and goals.

When we commit to a partnership, we commit to embracing each other's differences, and to working through the inevitable conflicts that will arise because of them. We agree as well to value the moments when we disagree, in the knowledge that by working out our differences we will be able to arrive together at a place that neither of us could have gotten to on our own. Finally, we delight in the security of knowing that we both value the same things and are working together to achieve a shared goal.

You Fall for Them Again

Needless to say, relationships don't come together so tidily. We move in and out of infatuation and reality, grief and partnership. Around and around it goes, in the workplace and in our personal lives—moments of excitement and peace, countered by moments of frustration and angst.

Such is the nature of relationships. Sigh!

Day Fourteen Action

Think about one or two of your most important platonic workplace relationships. What stage are you at with them—infatuation, reality, grief or partnership?

Notice who in these relationships is in the infatuation stage and who is experiencing the reality stage. Who is engaged in mirroring, and who is frustrated, and nagging for behavioral change?

Manage Primitive Impulses Now
Conscious Collective

Eventually, you will need to move to a stage of conscious partnership with your very close, long-term relationships. This means you will need to talk to people about how you work together, to help you negotiate a social contract around this partnership.

(continued)

(continued)

It's a good idea to discuss how you can best partner with each other, and define ways to tell each other when things are not going as you would like; finally, agree on how to respond to all of that.

If you revisit the scenario at the start of this chapter; before your reptilian brain steams ahead and tells you to fire the new hire, maybe you should take a moment, sit down with the person, and talk frankly about exactly how work is going for you both, and where you see it going in the future.

Week III

Tribe

Stakes in the Ground

> To be successful you have to be selfish, or else you never achieve. And once you get to your highest level, then you have to be unselfish. Stay reachable. Stay in touch. Don't isolate.
>
> —Michael Jordan

People: Can't live with them, can't live without them! Day in, day out, we continually swing back and forth between wanting to be on our own and be with others.

Some of us seem only able to function *outside* of a social group—the reclusive quiet types, outliers, rebels or sociopaths. Others of us need to be right in the thick of the group—the leaders, hangers-on, welcome participants.

Ayn Rand, the controversial and politically influential novelist, playwright, and Objectivist philosopher, emphasized relying on what actually exists, rather than on our feelings, in attempting to define our world. She wrote in her book *Philosophy: Who Needs It?* about the selfish nature of people: "Some are lone wolves (stressing that species' most predatory characteristics)... rejected by the tribe (or by the people of their immediate environment); they are too unreliable to

151

abide by conventional rules, and too crudely manipulative to compete for tribal power."

This nonconformist, or politically simplistic, way of surviving can lead us to drift from group to group, displaying what can look like a selfish need to cling to people and manipulate them.

If we are to work successfully in groups, it is essential that we develop a sense of our "self." Without the ability to understand ourselves and the values that make us who we are, we have an almost zero chance of meeting up with others who share our values and beliefs.

Strong social groups stay dedicated to their values. They do not change year in and year out, and do not bend to fit the day-to-day whims of individuals. It may be that that unbending nature causes many of us to avoid permanent commitment to a group; yet at the same time, we are compelled to desire acceptance from a community. Quite a conundrum!

Looking at this issue in the workplace, how do we simultaneously work within a team in order to hold onto the advantages that come from being social and, at the same time, maintain our independence?

Day 15

We Are Tribal

All Together Now . . .

Ora no Azu nwa.

—Igbo proverb

Today you'll tame:

♦ That lot—over there! Them!

Some probably find the Walmart cheer—which Sam Walton, the company founder, wrote—cultish and freaky. Others probably find it embarrassing. Yet many may find it motivating. However you feel about it, if you want to join the tribe at Walmart, or get inside the head of a "Walmartian," then you had better:

Give me a W! Give me an A! Give me an L!
Give me a squiggly!
Give me an M! Give me an A! Give me an R! Give me a T!
What's that spell?

(*continued*)

> (*continued*)
>
>   Walmart!
>   Whose Walmart is it?
>   It's my Walmart!
>   Who's number one?
>   The customer! Always!

Tribe: Call it a clan, a gang, a network, a family, or a company; whatever you call it, whoever you are, tribes are everywhere. In groups, companies, departments, teams, markets, professional disciplines—anywhere people with a common purpose or common experience gather—tribal behaviors will certainly be on display.

And wherever there is a tribe, there will be those excluded from it, bound up with all the ill feeling and impulsive behavior that results from that. You may be working in a team or a group or a company that doesn't "get" you; and you don't "get" them. Perhaps this is evident from the in-jokes told, shorthand spoken, and acronyms used, mutual understanding of certain business practices, and so on; some or all of which cause you on a very basic level to feel uncomfortable, intimidated, annoyed, given the cold shoulder, or put out to pasture.

How can you better navigate primitive tribal behaviors and penetrate tribal ranks to gain acceptance—that is, if you want to?

Club

Identifying the tribe or tribes with whom you work, and understanding and accepting their behaviors, is essential to getting along with them on the job. This is because every tribe has rules around how its members are expected to behave and interact. Every tribe shares *values, beliefs, rituals, customs, goals, concerns,* and *signals* that drive and shape how they behave within the external forces of their environment.

Tribal Makeup

Tribes consist of:

- *Values:* what they feel is most important in life
- *Beliefs:* the things they "just know," without needing any evidence to prove them
- *Rituals:* organized activities they do together on a regular basis to support their values and beliefs
- *Customs:* cultural practices they all share (such as the clothes they wear and the food they eat).
- *Goals:* objectives they set out to achieve together.
- *Concerns:* shared problems and conflicts
- *Signals:* specific ways they communicate with each other; may be a language or dialect, acronyms, vocabulary, even objects and symbols understood by the group alone.

Tribal behaviors often reveal the relative rank or social status of each member, and so can help you understand the influence each may have.

Working within a tribe's rules and hierarchy, and following established "normal" behaviors, can ensure you achieve a status within the group that will allow you to gain respect and have influence within the tribe, for at least a short time, and in some cases, for the rest of your professional and even personal life.

Functioning outside of the rules, hierarchy, and behavior of the tribe can, on the other hand, put you on the fast track to expulsion from the group!

First Tribe

From the day we are conceived, we become members of a tribe.

Our first tribe is the family we are born into; as we grow, we join other tribes—kids in nursery school or daycare; friends in the neighborhood; athletic teams; school groups and classes; fraternities or sororities; workplaces; social, religious, political, and user groups; and on and on.

You are likely a member of a number of tribes—a trade or profession, your company department, the softball or hockey team, the weavers' guild, an online gaming community, or other special interest group. You're even in a tribe with those who drive the same model car, motorcycle, or skateboard; take the same subway or highway into work; perhaps you listen to a "tribal leader" on drive-time radio. Chances are you belong to some tribes without even being aware of it.

You may think you don't belong to any tribes, that you are one of those individuals who does things on your own, in your own way, bucking the system, and setting the trends. Well, guess what, there are many more just like you out there, some of whom are reading this book, just like you, and thinking about it in the way you are now.

How very individual we all are!

Community Spirit

The Igbo proverb at the start of this chapter translates to: "It takes a village to raise a child."

Most of us need a tribe that is bigger than our families if we are going to survive to adulthood. How many of us have, for example, been rescued by a neighbor from an aggressive dog or bully that followed us down our street; or let us in when we lost our keys, and let us stay with them until Mom or Dad came home? How many of us were taken to task by that same neighbor when we held a party while we were home alone for the weekend? How many of us were visited in hospital by those same neighbors?

Today, "villages" take many forms: neighborhoods, recreational centers, companies we work for, professional organizations that certify our expertise, and many more. At a primitive level, all of these communities improve our likelihood of surviving.

Even industries work in extended villages as suppliers, partners, customers, and so on. It is difficult to do business with a village to which you are not connected. Imagine trying to open in a foreign market where you have no initial contacts. Or try switching professions with no friends, family, or colleagues in that area of work. Ask a new immigrant how successful he is in his job search in the absence of a "village" of friendly contacts in his adopted country to help him get his foot in the door.

Group-Work

In the business world, we often refer to villages as our "networks." Business networks are very important to us. They are composed of the first people we call to announce a new product or ask for help with a difficult problem.

We know intuitively that getting insight from those in our tribe will improve our chances of success, whether we are lost in the wilderness of northern Canada, floating on a raft in the Pacific Ocean, or trying to make a go of it in a career or business venture.

More people means more hands, more brainpower, more talent, different viewpoints and experience—all of which maximize our chances of making it in this challenging world. If you don't believe this, try cold-call selling for a living, as opposed to being able to reach out to your network for referrals.

Reptilian Brain Tribes

As I've said before, snakes, lizards, and frogs don't hang out together. We may at times find hundreds of them in the same location, but only because there is a lot of food and chances to mate there. They are not chatting about the harvest, stock prices, who makes the best cupcakes, or what the VP of Insect Acquisition said to the manager of Guano Disposal. They are not social beings. They do not cooperate with each other on future projects; nor do they celebrate or bemoan past ones.

Simply, most reptiles don't have a limbic system, that part of our primitive brain that is social. All humans do, as do all animals that raise their young and congregate in flocks, herds, prides, gaggles, and gangs.

Snakes lay eggs and slither away; and if the adults return after the young have hatched, they may even eat them. They are what we would consider "psychopathic" in human terms.

Animals with limbic systems, on the other hand, give birth to young who need nurturing and caretaking from the adults in the tribe. In the case of humans, this caretaking goes on for years.

Tribal by Nature

Humans are "hardwired" from birth to live, work, and play in tribes. In that way, we are all similar. But that's where the similarity ends.

The part of the world we live in, or have lived in, the religion our parents practiced, the neighborhood where the family home was located, the school we went to, who we hung out with as kids, and who we work for and with, all influence how we understand tribes. Furthermore, all these groupings influence which tribe(s) we seek to be a part of as adults.

Our first tribes informed and imprinted us with our initial set of shared values, beliefs, rituals, customs, goals, concerns, and signals. From these first tribes, our limbic brain was programmed neurologically with the behaviors we should and should not exhibit to remain in good standing with the tribe. We learned about our culture—the spoken and unspoken rules, traditions, stories, myths, music, and literature—which we have either maintained, rebelled against, or adapted and morphed together with the cultural elements of other tribes we have become part of in our adult lives.

Day Fifteen Action

Make a list of the tribes you are part of. (Keep this list in a safe place; you will need it again in a couple of days' time.) Think about more than the most obvious tribes you belong to, but also of the ones you are a unknown member of—perhaps so unknown that you have not even told yourself.

Consider the effects of tribal behavior at work. Do you exhibit some tribal behaviors that cause conflict with others? Is there a tribe you are a part of that seems to be in conflict with another? Are there feuding groups, like management versus workers or sales versus delivery? Or do you think that some tribes don't even realize they belong to clashing factions?

Tribes sometimes believe others are "wrong," rather than recognizing that because someone is an engineer, an accountant, or an HR professional—that is, members of those various work tribes—they may have some very different views of the world, and so some very different behaviors from each other. As the social psychologist David G. Myers says: "There is an objective reality out there, but we view it through the spectacles of our beliefs, attitudes, and values."

Manage Primitive Impulses Now
Tribal Warfare

When you come in contention with another person at work, think about the values and beliefs that may be driving any behavior that conflicts with your goals. Now think how you might be able to accept the values and beliefs of the other person or group. Once you understand and accept these values and beliefs, you may be able to better negotiate the difficult behavior.

Day 16

Tribal Nurture

Connected by Brood

Invisible threads are the strongest ties.

—Friedrich Nietzsche

Today you'll tame:

♦ The underlying misalignments

I joined the organization because it valued what it called "sky's-the-limit" thinking.

I loved that value. It fit with the way that I wanted to work, with an emphasis on innovation, creativity, and mobility around the organization. But I soon found out that it meant different things in different parts of the organization, and to different people within it.

One of these differences seemed to suggest to sales that they could make up a product, sell it to a client, and then leave everyone else to clean up the mess when they were unable to deliver it. It became clear the day that the FBI escorted our CFO out of the office that he had

(continued)

(*continued*)

been living the "sky's the limit" value in a very different way from that which the U.S. Securities and Exchange Commission deemed to be acceptable.

Our tribe was not one big happy family; rather, we were members in a loose collective of competing gangs—with some sick loners thrown in for good measure!

We learn about tribes from our first one: our family. For some, that tribe is a safe haven, a place of comfort and love; others, sadly, come to know their familial tribe as a source of pain and danger. As can sometimes happen in our first family tribe, sometimes our organizational tribe gets "sick," too—fragmented in some way. On the surface, it may look cohesive and healthy, but deep down it is troubled by infighting. Under these conditions we may find a culture marked by fear and intimidation, and within which we feel powerless and angry. It becomes hard for us to go to work every day, fearing that if we open our mouth to speak about the rot that has set into the tribe, the tribe will fire us! How can we possibly manage the conflict of being at war with our own tribe?

Fit

If we add our interactions from the neighborhood where we grew up together with those from school, it's easy to see why and how we each have our own unique experiences. There is good evidence that we develop our unconscious beliefs about the world and how it works during childhood. No wonder, then, that we often bring radically different perspectives to the tribes in which we did not grow up.

See if this story resonates with you: Maran was promoted through the ranks at his company, from the front lines (where he did blue-collar work) to assembly team supervisor and then to the manager of a group of engineers. After six months, his GM told him that his fellow managers didn't see him as a team player. Maran was blown away. He was well-liked at work, and thought that he had pretty good interpersonal skills. He had always played team sports, and was still playing hockey at age 40 with a bunch of "old boys" every Sunday at 6:00 AM. And he made sure to stay in touch with old friends he had worked with before he had moved on into different roles.

The problem was that Maran's work tribe still was his old blue-collar buddies, as these were the people with whom he felt most comfortable. He'd drop by their workstations during the day to chat, eat lunch with them, and connect with them on the weekends. He didn't feel like he was part of the managers' tribe, and so he didn't make an effort to connect with them. He never stopped by their offices to chat informally, eat lunch with them, or spend time with them after work or on the weekends. He simply didn't know how to be part of that tribe.

When Maran's GM reviewed the issues from a tribal perspective, he realized that he had not done anything to "induct" Maran into the managerial tribe. His solution was to give Maran a corporate credit card and assign him the "task" of taking each of his fellow managers out for lunch over the next two months. While at these lunchtime get-togethers, Maran was instructed to find out about each manager's interests, family, schooling, and so on—in addition to discussing business.

Most of us are exactly like Maran. We "fall" into tribes that offer a comfortable landing place for us, most of the time never realizing that we are fulfilling a destiny, or inevitability, one mapped out for us long before adulthood. Some of us are comfortable engaging in competitive sports; others shy away from such contests. Some are comforted by the structure and rituals of such groups as Toastmasters, Masons, or bowling leagues, while others find their formalities stifling to their abilities, conversation, or creativity.

Whichever tribe we end up being part of, we will be most successful as a member if we share its values and beliefs. If we don't, then we often end up trying to change the tribe—which causes its other members to regard us as a trouble-maker. Eventually, this usually either prompts us to leave of our own accord or we are asked to leave.

Values go way beyond qualities like honesty, civility, and so on. Our values are apparent in everything we do, from the clothes we put on in the morning to the way we style our hair or shave our face to the conversations we have and the behaviors we exhibit, or do not exhibit. Whether you know it or not, the rest of the tribe will know whether you share their values by all that you do. Just notice the next time a Jeep Wrangler drives by. Are you part of that tribe? Is the BMW convertible owner one of your fellow tribe members? Or perhaps cars are not important to you, but your bike, canoe, sailboat, subway, or daily walk to work indicate a tribe to which you belong.

Defining Our Values

Our values are those things that we deem most impor-tant to us. They are elements of the principles by which we run our lives.

Values are *conceptual*—things like family, equality, honesty, nature, education, perseverance, loyalty, faith-fulness. The list is probably endless. And even though we may not always live up to them, they set the bar for us, and we strive to reach it.

Our inventory of values is a very individualized listing; however, we share a lot of them based on the groups with which we have an affinity, belong to, or aspire to be a part of. We formed this list when we were young and still dependent on others around us for survival. We watched those around us who held resources vital to our well-being (not only food, water, light, and shelter, but social status—friends and followers) and mirrored their behavior, sometimes consciously, but mostly subconsciously.

This repetitive process—which goes on during our most formative years—establishes many of the neural pathways in our limbic brain. These pathways are then ready to fire as soon as we come into contact with a best-fit scenario.

This means we have strong connections in our brain that are just waiting to respond, like an Olympic athlete who is ready, set, and waiting for the sound of the starting pistol. Even the slightest movement on the trigger (the slightest hint of a minimum specification for what the neural pathway is expecting to detect) and you're off!

One way to predict, and then best manage our future actions, is to identify our values. Most decisions we make are based on these values; we either use them to tell us what to avoid or detest, what to desire and aspire to, and consequently, which groups to join and the groups to stay away from or attack.

Propaganda

How will we determine whether we'll fit in with the tribe in the workplace? Do we read the company website, listen to the leader speak, and get a "feeling" for her and the organization? Often, such communications will not reveal the true nature of the tribe, but only the external story (often, brand identity) the company wants its audience to perceive.

For example, let's take a look at the following values listed on a corporate website:

> *At the essence of the company stands its core value of understanding the needs of its four constituents: Colleagues, Customers, Company, and Community. We invite and encourage every colleague to live these values—what we call "standing in the circle." In doing so, we can fulfill our mission of becoming the most admired card and lending business in the world.*

This all sounds highly laudable. This company also states its beliefs as: "great leadership and teamwork," "great behaviors," "respect, trust," and the corporate staple, "integrity."

In practice, however, it is clear that Barclays Bank, from whose 2012 website these quotes were taken, has not displayed behaviors that support these values and beliefs during the early twenty-first century. Some people, including the company's former head, have gone so far as to call the bank's behaviors "reprehensible." A senior employee spoke of a "culture of fear" on the trading floor, one that led to rigging rates and, potentially, defrauding others in the banking community. The most damning accusation was that a "management by intimidation" culture existed, which ensured no one would blow the whistle on behavior that was out of sync with the published tribal values and beliefs.

By now the Barclays story reads like an all-too-common corporate tale, one revealing that some of the company tribe's real behavior doesn't even come close to resembling that which it presents to the world.

Our primitive tribal brain's limbic system will often come into conflict with any group that does not live up to the values that it holds dear. It will also give others who do not adhere to our values a bad reputation; and the primitive social brains of others will do the same about us. Beware!

Day Sixteen Action

Ask a few people at work to describe your tribe's values—whether it represents your whole company, your division, or only a team you are a member of. Inquire as well as to what behaviors you and others in your company exhibit that reflect these values. Are these the values you want for your tribe? Is this the tribe you initially felt you had joined? If not, what behaviors do you all need to change to get in sync with your shared values? How can you replace the inappropriate behavior with another that *does* uphold the values (and reputation) you want to have and maintain?

Manage Primitive Impulses Now
Not What They Expected?

Groups may be presented to you as having a certain "brand." Either colleagues will tell you how the tribe you are about to meet will perform; or you may, on your own, find that the tribe members themselves deliver to you a very clear message about what you should expect from them.

What you hear and what you experience may be two different things, and this can cause conflict, disappointment, surprise, or confusion for you. Understand that it is the same for others who meet your tribe. They have been told to expect a certain behavior, which they may or may not get.

If others appear angry, let-down, shocked, or baffled by what your group is doing, you might ask them what they were expecting and hoping for, and what they feel they have gotten instead. With this information, you can begin to think about how you might realign the behaviors of the group to meet what others expected of it.

Day 17

Hierarchy

No Such Thing as a Flat Organization

Every employee tends to rise to his level of incompetence.
—Dr. Laurence J. Peter

Today you'll tame:
◆ The urge to climb to the top of the heap

The Information Technology restructure project was an important one, and needed a new approach. The boss had just come back from a retreat where he'd been completely star-struck by a business guru's latest thinking on Organizational Design, where companies would work toward leveling out hierarchies in the workplace. Before taking any time to properly process what he'd heard, and think more carefully about if this ideal could effectively be applied to his company's current circumstances, he sent an announcement to his entire organization, which read as follows:

> *We are putting together a completely self-managed, elite team. It's based on total autonomy of the individual*

contributor. You will self-select to join with an open-door policy; if you aren't contributing fully, then you should take time out. Never move forward without 100% concordance on any decisions.

In turn, a large number of the employees self-elected themselves to sign up, as per this instruction. In the days that followed, scheduling any kind of team meeting for this group became impossible—individuals opted instead to participate in splinter group meetings that took place among like-minded factions. Individual members of these factions would then approach the boss for signoff on their clique's decisions.

Amongst this confusion, one of the key technical leads (often shy, and seemingly a little fragile) quit the project in favor of joining a part of the company that adhered to a classic management structure and strict timelines. Another employee, considered "high-potential," who believed she was a shoo-in for a leadership position, quit the company in disgust, and went to work for a competitor.

The boss, noticing after a month into his new organizational regime, that nothing about the project had moved forward, lay down the law "old style" to the team saying "Lock yourselves in a room for a day and sort this !@#$ out. Nisha—you're in charge!" They quickly re-ordered their group, assigning various members responsibility for key areas of organization, while establishing clear shared goals.

While they incorporated into their plan the new idealistic values set out by their leader around the importance of self-determination and freedom, by distributing clear areas of responsibility and accountability to the group's members, they effectively reinstated a hierarchical structure. At that point, the project started to move along at a pace.

Our primitive brains conduct status checks all the time, leading us, for example, to ask people when we first meet them, "What do you do?," when what we really want to know is do they have more power than us?

Talk about our holiday in the Caribbean, to try and find out whether they are richer than we are.

Ask about a colleague's new car, even as we wonder, will he get more attention from the guys?

And on and on.

In short, tribes are hierarchical. With this comes our personal impulse to gain an advantage in that hierarchy, by putting others down or clinging more tightly to our positions, even as others are inevitably doing the same to us.

When a group of people from different departments in a company sit down for a meeting, you can be sure that each is unconsciously noting where he or she fits within the hierarchy. If they are jockeying for position, it is often to gain more recognition or more power, or to be seen as "buddies" with those who have the power.

Symbols

What one tribe values or believes to be powerful may not have the same value for other tribes. Which means that the visible symbols one tribe uses as indicators of power may not "ring the same bells"; have the same connotations for members of another group. For example, the four stars alongside your name on your ID badge will have a different meaning if you're a Marine than if you work for McDonald's; and may have no meaning at all within another organization. In some cases, symbols that denote value or power in one group may even have the reverse meaning, thus demoting you in the eyes of another. (Chocolate money gives me a high rank with my kids, yet at the bank makes me look like a fool.)

Alpha–Beta–Omega

That said, all tribes including work tribes have some similar primitive currencies that clearly signal rank. You may find that the alpha (i.e., dominant) person in any one group takes up a lot of "territory," in terms of both time and space. Alphas tend to gravitate toward the ends of the table, the positions of control, with easy lines of sight to everyone and important resources. You won't often find an alpha sitting with his back to a main entrance way, for instance.

Furthermore, tribal hierarchies function somewhat like a wolf pack, where rank order is maintained through ritualized posturing. Psychological warfare is preferable to physical confrontation, which means that high-ranking status is based more on personality or attitude than on size or physical strength. And just as in a wolf pack, in human hierarchies there are those who are kept at the bottom of the pecking order: the omegas who absorb aggression from the rest of the pack and are used to stabilize the relationships between the alpha (usually, one of the parents of the pack when it comes to wolves) and the betas (most often, their progeny).

Kicking Post

Individuals in some tribes are invited into a tribal den simply to serve as omegas, the punching bags upon which the alpha and betas can safely take out their aggression and then send them packing.

Many of us have found ourselves inadvertently in this position at some point—and you probably don't want to be there more than once with the same gang! That said, there is a somewhat constructive way to look at this situation: At least when you occupy this position, you are in the tribe, albeit very low down in its ranks. Indeed, sometimes this position serves as the entry point to a tribe; you are a rookie, an apprentice, an intern, a greenhorn. Your next step is to work your way up to beta level.

Top Down

The tribe will often collude unconsciously to make the negative (on occasion, quite insane looking) behaviors of its alpha appear totally acceptable. The tribe might even allow him to bully others or act out in ways that anyone else would immediately judge as immoral or, in some cases, illegal. The betas will rarely attempt to challenge or threaten the alpha, either physically or metaphorically—*unless* they are making a play for the alpha position.

If, however, one of the betas accidently destabilizes the alpha, both the alpha and the rest of the pack may regard this as a play for the top-ranking position. In these cases, other tribe members may attack the beta and then ostracize him from the pack, for a while. In professional scenarios, this might translate to being left out of project meetings, taken off the e-mail routing list, or being made to feel unwelcome around the coffee table at break time.

Will the pack realize they are excluding the beta in these cases? Interestingly, they might not, for the simple reason it is easier for the primitive brain to quickly decide that the person is "mad or bad," and that he is losing his grip on the tribe's "code of behavior" within the society, or that he has purposely decided to destabilize the group and make a power move. Some group members may even believe the beta is colluding with a competitive, "enemy," tribe.

Treading on Toes

We have all been guilty of inadvertently treading on the toes of a tribe's ranking member, and been (sometimes quite literally) "sent to Siberia," either temporarily or permanently, depending on the severity of the "injury." (I heard that one VP of an oil company who made what was perceived as a power play on the CEO was instantly relocated to one of the company's Caspian Sea projects.) We have all failed to get the promotion we thought was a sure thing, or make the big sale, or be invited to a pivotal meeting, simply because we did not pay close enough attention to the signals we needed to send within the tribe, especially those that show we accept and respect the social ranking in place.

Take this story as an example: Jed was feeling good. A mutual client had introduced him to Ushi, the VP of a financial services company, and they had taken an instant liking to each other. Over coffee, they chatted about some of the dilemmas Ushi's company faced, after which Jed offered his thoughts on how his company's service address them. Ushi then told Jed that she was sure that Carlos, the president of her company, would be interested in his ideas as well, and offered to introduce the two of them. Jed was confident about his industry knowledge, and appreciated Ushi's enthusiasm. The meeting with Carlos and Ushi went well, too, with the president becoming quite animated during their discussion. When, near the close of the meeting, Carlos laid out his plan involving Jed's company, Jed listened carefully, before replying, "That sounds good, Carlos, but I would suggest a different approach," which he then went on to outline. Ushi and Carlos listened quietly, and raised no objections before they closed the session. It was only later, when neither Ushi nor Carlos had replied to Jed's follow-up e-mails, that he began to wonder if something had gone wrong, and if so, what.

As we know, tribes are hierarchical. In this case, Jed was to learn the hard way that there was room for only one alpha in Ushi's company, and Carlos was that one. Ushi, of course, knew this; and though she was given a great deal of autonomy within the company, she was careful never to challenge Carlos's status. Poor Jed, however, was also used to being an alpha in the tribes to which he belonged, and so he behaved that way. But laying out his own plan implied to Carlos that Jed thought his was a better plan.

At that precise moment, Jed lost the sale.

Patterns and Position

The position you held in your family hierarchy, your class at school, or among your group of friends, college classmates, and others may have influenced what you see as your place today within your professional and personal tribes. Naturally, you won't necessarily, or even likely, be at the same status level in the various tribes in which you are a member. You may be most comfortable as a follower in some tribes, even when you expect or demand to be the leader in others.

Joining a new tribe always offers the opportunity to assess where you might be able to move to within the hierarchy, regardless of the position you hold or held in other teams, groups, or companies. Those of you with an entrepreneurial spirit may decide that "I can be the boss of me!" You may thus decide to break free of the confinement you feel working for "the Man" and step out on your own.

Ordo Ab Chao

Why do we collude with primitive hierarchical tribal behaviors? Well, in part because the alternative is interpreted by the primitive brain as chaos. Even the most independent and entrepreneurial-minded individuals tend to place themselves within a group, or look up to role models whose values and beliefs they share. The reason for this can be found in the evolutionary advantage of the hierarchical structure; it is programmed into our primitive brain via our dopamine-driven "approach or avoid" system.

Plenty of forward-thinking management and organizational styles will not conform to these primitive systems. These can succeed only as long as the resource levels in the group are high and predictable, thereby keeping anxiety low. But if things get tough, resource levels drop dangerously low, and nobody quite knows who it taking responsibility for what, then all hell might break loose!

Day Seventeen Action

Knowing where you fit into the hierarchy, and being comfortable with your position, is crucial to being a successful member of the tribe. Think about the work tribes you are part of: Do you feel you are at a fair ranking in that tribe, given your assets and contributions, or do you feel you have not been fully recognized? If the latter, are you, or have you thought about, challenging anyone for leadership? Or are you ignoring or shunning anyone you regard as not worthy of your attention?

Members of a tribe (including you) can often tell whether others respect them or are shunning them, without it being made explicit. Being respected raises the level of dopamine in the body and makes people feel good; being shunned, on the other hand, lowers the level of this feel-good neurotransmitter causing behaviors of retreat or aggression.

How common does any of this behavior feel for you right now?

Manage Primitive Impulses Now
Give 'Em a Raise!

If you raise someone's rank, it's important to realize that it will affect the others around them. When you enhance one person's professional status, it may imply to others that they have been demoted. What might also happen is that by raising rank levels, the "currency" loses its value. Think about those companies in which almost everyone is a VP!

Day 18

Tension

Autonomy versus Belonging

Ich hab' noch einen Koffer in Berlin

—Marlene Dietrich

Today you'll tame:
◆ Sociopathic tendencies

Jane was irate. She had not been invited to the project meeting. It reminded her that this kind of thing had happened to her at her last company, too.

The reality was that there was no real need for her to be at the meeting, and her colleagues didn't want to waste her time. They knew she often was frustrated, complaining how busy and overrun with work she was. They didn't want to bother her.

Now, however, she was complaining loudly and aggressively to management about being sidelined on this project. She claimed the work would suffer without her insight and input.

Jane's "fit" prompted management to send an e-mail to the team leader, Robin, to the effect that Jane was upset, and that she, and they, blamed him for putting her in this mood, by excluding her from the group. Robin, in turn, sent a message to Jane—and copied the rest of the team—apologizing unreservedly for his oversight. He ended by including an invite to the next meeting, along with an agenda that listed Jane's input right at the top, as the first item.

The day of the meeting came around, and the group waited 10 minutes for Jane to arrive to kick it off, since she was first on the agenda.

She was a no-show.

Almost an hour later, they finally received a message from her that she was too busy to attend, and that their project was not a priority for her right now, as she had, that day, started a new one of her own. She would "rather not be bothered by any further requests to meet on this matter, unless absolutely essential."

The truth was, she had never even entered the meeting into her schedule in the first place.

Why is it that almost all end-of-the-world stories feature someone trying to survive alone while others are trying to make it as a team? During hard times, would you really want to strike out on your own, or seek out a strong group and hunker down with them?

Solo or Group

Remember, the same need for survival that causes our primitive reptilian brain to drive us to fend for ourselves also drives our more recently evolved (but still quite primitive, by 200 million years) limbic brain to be tribal, part of the gang. Both of these systems are judging the pros and cons of being social versus independent as if they were preparing for Armageddon, as opposed to the reality (e.g., prepping for the quarterly beer and pizza event or the monthly sales or weekly team meeting). The consequence of this internal battle between our reptilian "sociopath" and our limbic "socialite" can be impulsive behavior in the workplace—and thus hard to handle. Especially as, when certain colleagues are prone to antisocial behaviors, they can be slippery as snakes.

Here are some of the benefits the reptilian brain sees of going solo:

- I can move faster.
- I will need fewer resources.
- I'll be stealthier.
- I'll face less conflict.

Meanwhile, the limbic system is thinking of the cons of going it alone:

- There'll be no one to look after me.
- I'll be lonely.
- It'll be depressing.
- I'll feel less secure.

Then it considers the pros of teaming up:

- I'll get group support.
- I'll have extra resources.
- I'll have less work to do.
- I'll feel more secure.

Under pressure, the reptilian brain sees only the uncertainties involved in teaming up, and asks:

- Can I trust these other people?
- Is this a winning team?

And the most pressing question:

◆ Will I get lunch?

There really is no middle ground here. You are either part of a group or you aren't. The moment you stop going solo, you become partly responsible to everyone else in the group—all of whom are likewise responsible to you. You're in a collective. Sometimes this feels safe, and sometimes very dangerous—just as when you go it alone.

Regardless of which option you choose, and when, you and others will judge the choice you make, both as individuals and as a group. This can be a problem, because some people value individualism, and so view choosing the "lone wolf" option as acceptable, while others, those who place a higher value on collectivism, might view this choice with suspicion.

Parties

Individualism and collectivism represent conflicting viewpoints about or beliefs in human nature, society, and the relationship between them.

Individualism says that being an individual is the highest standard of value. It does not, however, hold that groups should not exist, or that teams are not useful; rather that any society is a collection of individuals and, most importantly, that society as a whole should not be valued over and above them.

In contrast, supporters of collectivism view the group as the most important construct in society. Collectivists maintain that individual identity is determined by the groups, within which each of us interacts. Further, collectivism holds that we are defined by our relationships with others.

In sum, individualists see people dealing primarily with their separate realities, and that other people are just one aspect of those realities. Whereas collectivists regard people as dealing primarily with other people, and that the individual's reality is only a by-product of that. It is at this point that the distinction between the two can start to sound less philosophical and more moralistic: Individualism holds that every person is an end unto him—or herself, and that no one should be sacrificed for the sake of another; collectivism holds that the individual's needs and goals are subordinate to the larger group—in other words, the individual's needs *should* be sacrificed when the collective requires it.

You will not be surprised to learn that the two viewpoints have been debated for hundreds of years, by those who study ethics and politics—not to mention more than a few episodes of *Star Trek*. The right and wrong of "being part of the group" versus "being in it for yourself" has been a resonant theme throughout all of recorded history. Consequently, it can be judged as an ongoing battle between our reptilian primitive brain, which is in it only for us, and our limbic, social primitive brain, which is in it for our tribe.

Take, for example, the infamous declaration of an admirer of Ayn Rand and former British Prime Minister Margaret Thatcher: "There's no such thing as society. There are individual men and women, and there are families." If this were a logical statement, it begs the question who on earth Mrs. Thatcher believed she was governing. We can only put down this statement to her individualistic values and beliefs.

Thank God for Richard Dawkins

As you recall, our beliefs are the assumptions we make about the world. They grow from what we see, hear, experience, read, and think about. They apply not only how we see ourselves but also how we assess other people. We tend not to question our beliefs once we've made them, because we are so certain they are correct.

Therefore, we tend to think we do not need reliable data to support our beliefs, so when someone offers information that conflicts with what we believe, we may have a quite violent reaction against the information or the person supplying it.

Like values, many of our beliefs stem from the most formative years of our brain's development, as we witnessed the world around us and determined how, from our limited viewpoint, it seemed to function. Our brains formed strong neural pathways based on these repetitive experiences. We maintain these, in a very physical way; they become our "universal laws," which we then apply to new situations.

The evolutionary benefit of this development is that we do not have to think so much. We simply *react* to our environment, and to those in it, which from an energy standpoint is highly cost-effective.

Here's a personal example: My experience of family, education, and popular media during my childhood all contributed, laid the pathway in other words, to the forming of my own belief that many of Darwin's theories, as well as those of many subsequent theoreticians on the evolutionary process via natural selection, are correct. Logically, I realize that these ideas are "just" theories; but they have been substantiated by enough well-researched data that I am convinced they are valid; I agree with them; they feel like "the truth" to me.

Other people I hang around with believe so much more strongly than I do in evolutionary theory that if I say, for example, that evolution "*may* be a fact," they rebut vehemently, "But it *is fact*!!!" And I find it hard to disagree with them; it even becomes socially awkward for me to revert to my more logical position that

(*continued*)

> (*continued*)
>
> "evolution currently sounds to me like the most probable theory for our biological world," rather than expressing the tribal belief that "We should take evolution as a given." It is much easier just to nod my head and say, "Yes, I know; I'm just arguing for the sake of it—for sport," and then take a sip of my beer and suggest to my friends, "Let's talk about neuroactive peptides instead!" (By the way, should you ever wish to join us, we meet at the Newt & Badger in Pedantville every Thursday. Bring a working knowledge of organic chemistry.)

Isolation

The fact that individualism means, in part, "being alone" frequently prompts people to say that being an individual is incompatible with being cooperative. In other words, a person who is too much of an individualist is often viewed as not a team player. Yet often in business, the person who would rather do things her own way is not typically branded as antisocial; rather she is regarded a "natural leader" or "self-starter"—if, to some, a closed-minded one.

Evolution has proven that by cooperating with other people we gain tremendous advantage in terms of our chances of survival. Individualism does not negate this. Certainly, not all collective living and working arrangements are beneficial to the individual; consider one such enforced arrangement, that of American slaves.

Only when your rational neocortex examines both the benefits and disadvantages of belonging to all of the tribes to which you currently belong, versus those benefits and disadvantages of moving toward your goals on your own terms, can you truly measure the extent of your innate desire to join with others, versus heading out on your own—sometimes to your advantage and sometimes to your detriment.

Responsibility versus the Safety Net

The primal pull between the individual and the group has, over time, been reflected in the values and beliefs regarding how we head out on our own or work together in groups. These values and beliefs govern our behavior when we see others breaking away from the team or pulling together with it. They also prompt some positive feelings about attending to our own groups, as well as some guilt when we opt out of them.

This conflict is clearly apparent in the workplace, since a primary element of individualism is *individual responsibility*. Being responsible is one way of being proactive, making one's choices consciously and carefully, and accepting accountability for all one does—or fails to do. A measure of taking responsibility at work is what is commonly known as *productivity*. You have to "earn your way" and "pull your weight." There is no room for slackers!

Collectivism frames any failure to be self-supportive, a "social problem" that society has to deal with. This is often framed in the workplace as a "structural problem within the organization" or the "wrong environment" for the individual worker (i.e., having "the right person in the wrong job"). Thus, collectivists may seek to weave a social safety net, to protect individuals from the choices they make.

Within the context of work, we might often face dilemmas stemming from the extent to which we believe our organization should act as a safety net for unproductive individuals, or perhaps negative behaviors; and to what extent we should view this as *entirely* the individual's responsibility. Our response to some group behaviors will be based on our own tribal biases, in favor of or against, individualism and collectivism.

For example, the entrepreneurial head of a company, who may value individualism highly, might preach to her unproductive team to "look to yourselves, be your own personal best and better than the person next to you." In contrast, this company's HR manager, who values collectivism and feels the business should "respect the needs of the group to work within their abilities," might tell the company to "pull together, don't leave anybody behind for dead . . . even if we don't hit our targets for this year, at least we'll go into next year as a stronger team!" This latter mind-set however can clearly result in an altruistic management style, at odds with the entrepreneurial business owner's goal for growth in their company.

My Brother's Keeper

Altruism should not be mistaken for kindness, generosity, and the desire to help other people along. It is more than these. Altruism *demands* self-sacrifice in its devotion to benefit others. The billionaire who contributes $50,000 to a charity fund is not necessarily acting only altruistically, since altruism goes beyond simple charity. Altruism requires forgoing one's own needs so that others may be more prosperous. A charitable workplace is one that gives its employees time off to visit loved ones in need, because it can afford do so. An altruistic workplace does the same, knowing also that its productivity might suffer because of it. It acts out of compassion and social responsibility.

Reasonable

The character judgments we might make about a person who joins in, versus sits out, are probably not at all reasonable and rational. We all harbor deep-seated expectations about what sort of person is private and what sort of person is social. Unfortunately, such black-and-white assessments keep us from appreciating the more complex and overriding fact that we humans work both in groups *and* as individuals; we voluntarily agree to interact, or to go our separate ways. This system has, however, some limits. At one end there is coercion to join, to "be a team player or clear out your desk"; at the other end is a "do what you like" attitude, and if we all gain from it then that's just a bonus.

Day Eighteen Action

What, in relation to the tribe, is the role you prefer? Are you more of a loner or a team player? And, how does the tribe view your position? Does it accept your choices to join in or to go it alone, or do the other members of the tribe view you with suspicion?

Friends "R" Us

Traditionally, tribes are on the smaller side; consider the family, village, council, or guild. It's only very recently that humans have become part of larger civilizations, and even more recently that it's been possible for many of us to use modern communications to sustain memberships with huge tribes over vast international and transglobal distances. Some might argue that these tribes are artificial: "How can you have 500 *friends*? That's ridiculous! There's no way you'll find me on Facebook." Whereas others will dismiss such talk as the small-minded ranting of a Luddite.

Pull out the list you made on Day Fifteen of tribes that you belong to (and keep it handy because you'll need it again next week). Notice how big they are. What size best suits you, and for what purposes? Are some too big to be useful; do they make you feel excluded or isolated? Or do they cause you to feel a little more individualistic about your relationship to them? Are others "just right" in size— you are comfortable in them, feel related to others and valued enough so that you can pull together to reach a common goal—maybe even "losing yourself" in it now and again?

Manage Primitive Impulses Now
The Selfish Gene

It's all too easy when someone is not being a team player to negatively judge her behavior as selfish, or even sociopathic. But before you solidify that judgment, why not ask her how the team could work better for her, and vice versa? Ask not what she can do for the team, but what the team can do for her. Try to figure out what the exchange would have to be in order to get her fully on board; then decide whether it would be worth it for the group, or if, as you first diagnosed, that would be making a bargain with a devil!

Day 19

Values

Diverging Opinions

> *"That was excellently observed," say I, when I read a passage by an author, where his opinion agrees with mine.*
> —Jonathan Swift

Today you'll tame:

- ◆ The subterranean chasms of trust between our groups

An international pharmaceutical company had gathered together both its Swedish and American representatives in the room. The objective was to work out how to align the North American and European strategies to achieve greater profitability.

Before they could make any strategic decisions together, however, one thing became clear: The very meeting tactics by which the two regional groups were attempting to make decisions beneficial to their respective groups and the company as a whole, were in no way aligned.

(continued)

(continued)

The Swedes preferred to follow the agenda point by point, each waiting his turn to speak, before reaching consensus via an orderly debate. The U.S. contingent wanted to skip areas that they did not regard as valuable, talk across each other, and then let their leader make a decision.

Consequently, both sides were becoming irritated; the meeting was devolving into dysfunction and disagreement on every point.

The Swedes valued consensus over hierarchy, while the Americans valued hierarchy over consensus. Both had perfectly reasonable ways of coming to a decision, but neither group had experience working in any other way than its own. Thus, neither could trust the other's process, and so trust the other party.

Putting the two teams together turned out to be a recipe for tribal disaster.

We humans have an innate tendency to perceive "reality" through the prism of our own values and beliefs. This inevitably shapes our attitude to the world around us—including our attitude toward people who both share our views and do not. We classify the people around us according to cultural "types" in order to judge quickly whether their attitudes align or are in conflict with ours—and, therefore, are safe or risky to be around. These cultural classifications ultimately drive whether we trust, and how we manage, those we work with.

Picture the following professionals (all male in this case) managing you on the job. Which one you would trust most?

- The casual manager, wearing a beard and an open-necked shirt
- The "smooth" manager, wearing trendy eyeglasses and designer clothes

- The businesslike manager, dressed in a traditional suit and tie
- The silver-haired manager, who looks more like a friendly advisor

Affiliations to Appearance

When we are judging who might be a good leader for us, isn't our first consideration what he *says*, rather than how he looks? And if not, shouldn't it be?

But it isn't always, because, as we've already discussed, we tend to treat a person's appearance—how he dresses, how attractive he is to us, the way he carries himself—as clues to his value system.

We expect the manager in the suit, for example, to be a man who believes individuals should stand on their own feet; whereas we perceive the guy with the beard to be someone who supports equality in the workplace. The designer type we think must be a cool individualist, in contrast to the older gentleman who must surely respect tradition. These types are, I realize, crude generalizations, adapted roughly from those used by researchers at Yale University's Cultural Cognition research project. *Cultural cognition* describes the tendency people have to form their perceptions mostly in keeping with their existing values and cultural types—of which appearance makes up a large part.

Which one did you pick out as the man you would like as your manager? Yale's research found that "suits" prefer to be managed by like-minded "suits"; employees with facial hair prefer managers in beards; and so on. Therefore, the manager you chose likely is a representation of *you*.

How do our tendencies to perceive others through the lens of our own values and cultural norms affect how manageable we are by them in the workplace? Well, there's a reason we generally react in a close-minded way when taking instructions from a manager: We fear the implications of the instruction; that once carried out, the result may pose a threat to us. However, if the instruction comes from someone who looks somehow like they *affirm* our values, we will take their direction in a much more open-minded way. Being receptive and agreeable to a manager's demands is an indication we identify with this person. We trust that the people we identify with are more likely to share our values; that they pose less of a risk to us and our tribe. Indeed, they look like the others in our tribe, and so we trust that they, too, are invested in our survival.

The way we dress and groom—display behaviors—is typically a clear signal that marks the tribe to which we belong and with which we identify.

More simply put, we tend to like the people who are like us—and their ideas, projects, and management. "Liking" is a major component of intimacy and bonding. The quicker we can get another to like us, the quicker we can (potentially) manage them.

Lazy Leader

I was president of an entrepreneurial business networking group for a year. This entailed leading a number of what are commonly referred to as A-type personalities toward a common goal. The parent organization for our chapter had developed a fairly hefty manual containing the rules for running such a group.

When it comes to reading a manual, I admit to being quite lazy. Not because I have any reliable data that says manuals are not helpful, but because my management style is, overall, quite lazy. I prefer to allow people to self-manage. Here, too, I don't have data informing me

---

that self-management is best for organizations. Again, it's just that I am inherently lazy when it comes to leading large groups; or maybe it is just very complex tasks that cause me to check out. Who knows? I'm also far too lazy to undertake an investigation to figure out this behavior.

Unfortunately, when I was working on this project, I was deluged every day with requests for judgments and rulings on the various actions and interactions taking place within the group. I calculated that if I actually took the time to fully understand the situation and think about the best approach, given all the facts, opinions, and beliefs, I would have no time to complete any other work I had committed to. (And let us not forget the laziness factor!)

So instead, I adhered to the one central core value and belief around which the group was convened—known as "Givers Gain"—and would reply to everyone's request for a ruling that they should do whatever caused them to "give and gain the most." Then I left it up to them to follow their own course of action.

Do you think this was good or lazy leadership, or both?

Valuing the Disagreement

Some will say that disagreement used to be valued more highly. They'll harken back to a time when you could have a good argument with someone, yet neither party's nose got out of joint.

Maybe this is true; maybe not.

Yet it often seems in this more liberal age that we are called upon at work to validate *everyone's* views. I'm guessing you have attended meetings where ignorance is taken for as valid a platform for discussion as informed intelligence. It's incumbent upon the group to invite all those involved in the issue, give them a say, and praise them, no matter their level of engagement, insight, or responsibility. And, probably, you've all been at meetings where the opinion of the uninformed is given as much credence as that of the expert. Not because a diversity of opinion leads to innovation, but out of fear of treading on the toes of others, who have lives as valid our own, despite the fact that they have as much to contribute to the meeting agenda as an amoeba. It can be incredibly annoying, to say the least, and a tremendous waste of time, when *everyone* around the table is asked to give their input about matters that concern only a few, or about which only a few have knowledge.

When, instead, there is informed dissent, when a person countering your thoughts helps you to refine them, challenge them, and figure them out, there is great value. Constructive disagreement, dialogue, and discussion are great ways of testing the status quo.

But when that happens, do we even bother to listen—really listen?

In many settings nowadays—including the workplace—any form of disagreement is taken as an offense. And those who disagree may be crushed, hidden, or persecuted.

The limbic, more social primitive brain seeks out like minds and conformity; seeing things differently is the domain of the neocortex. As a result, unless the neocortex is consciously switched on, to allow for dissenting opinions (thereby keeping the limbic brain at bay), "group-think" can be glorified above common sense, and blind compliance praised above and beyond rational dissent.

Remember that to the reptilian platform of our primitive brain, disagreement is a "best fit" to conflict. Our primitive brain computes: If disagreement, then enemy. For our limbic platform disagreement may mean a fight or it may mean a family, depending on the atmosphere you grew up in.

Our more modern rational neocortex can discern very easily that disagreement and conflict are not necessarily the same. However, our primitive modules are obsessed with the idea that like-minded people will accept us; and not only will that gang of like minds agree with us when we're among them, they will encourage us to stay on track. Thus, we seek them out and collaborate with them more often than we do with those who disagree with us. This is what makes it so tempting to quickly develop a *line of reason*, one that doesn't leave space or time for anything—or anyone—else.

Pedants

This is not to say that you should surround yourself with people who shoot down your every idea as though it's the most foolish thing they've ever heard. It is to say that if you are a leader with whom nobody ever disagrees, you are in a very precarious position, because blind compliance never lasts; people, at least some of them, will eventually regain their sight.

Day Nineteen Action

Resisting the seductive temptation to believe that you are a genius, and that everything you devise is brilliant, and that everyone should agree with you, is very difficult to do. Your primitive brain is addicted to the dopamine rush of the status gain that comes with this line of thought.

The first step in accepting the reality, that you aren't perfect, is challenging. To help meet that challenge, start today by seeking out opinions and viewpoints different from your own. Notice how open or closed you are to these ideas. Then take this a step further by coming up with and bringing forward some points that support the arguments of others.

For relationships and teams to succeed, it's important that the individuals in them share values. See if you can value diversity, and if the entire team can adopt this as one of their shared values.

If you practice being open to "the other," give him the benefit of the doubt and trust him more, you'll be less likely to face conflicts about the "stuff" that mattered hundreds of thousands of years ago, but no longer does in our modern work world.

Structure and Function

When it comes to helping diverse groups, like the Swedes and Americans in story at the start of the chapter, come to a consensus, it's a good idea to involve a third party to guide both sides in establishing mutual ground rules on how to go about reaching an agreement.

Manage Primitive Impulses Now
You're Welcome to Disagree

Embracing disagreement is an effective way to leverage your team's strengths and broaden your own thinking. You can stress the importance of balanced thinking by having some fun, by engaging in what I call the "YesState™." This is, simply, a state of mind you put yourself into consciously, which by default, is open and accepting of others, their ideas, opinions, and attitudes. This doesn't mean you believe or value what they believe and value, merely that you can *accept* it as important and valid to them.

When you do this, welcome the naysayers into the mix, and dismiss judgments that imply, for example, "They have lost the thread of this conversation completely," or "They are just trying to be disruptive." And when you realize that opinions about you or your work are negative, simply think to yourself, or even say out loud, "Yes," or "Okay," or "I see," or "I get it"—anything to indicate you accept the point of view. Then ask for more input on it. Doing so will offset your primitive brain's *default to the negative* tendency that can cause you to launch an immediate counterattack. Instead, you will allow your neocortex to think rationally about the opposing point to your ideas, view, or demands. If it turns out you hold to your original position, say so, but in a calm, respectful, yet assertive, manner, rather than in a rude, out-of-control whirlwind of primal impulse.

Day 20

Diversity
High-Performing Teams

True . . . there is no "I" in team, but there is a "u" in suck.
—Anonymous

Today you'll tame:
♦ Customarily avoiding the assortment

The change management company sent word out that they needed an injection of "creativity, zest, and life" to make it stand out in the marketplace.

One of my best friends and colleagues was hired to supply that boost of energy to the company. He was everything it needed: well-educated, smart, creative, and a live wire.

On his first day at the firm, he was pretty much stopped at the door and told to go and buy a dark suit before coming back to work—despite the fact that he had already toned down his usual "look" considerably.

Even after he returned more appropriately dressed, from the first moment, any ideas he brought to the table—which, by the way, had been highly successful in many other sectors—were shot down.

More puzzling to him was that the leader who had brought him in to update the company's approach to innovation instructed him *not* to do "any of that out-of-the-box @#$% here!" because theirs was a traditional company, driven by process metrics and hierarchy. The most positive responses my friend received to any of his proposals were, "We like what you've done. Now redo it so it is more like 'us.'" Even then, his work was never shown to any of the company's clients.

My friend believed he was being assigned only to "Siberian projects," those that were not important, where his work would have no effect. In short, he was prevented from doing exactly what he had been hired by the change management company to do.

The result: Everyone was stuck.

Yes, ironic!

The company missed out on my friend's value, and never did differentiate.

Notably, the company dissolved four years later. As for my friend, he founded one of the most innovative and successful companies that I work with.

Variety is far more than the spice of life; it is essential to its well-being. Biological biodiversity is the best example; the variation of life-forms within a given environment are the measure of that ecosystem's health. In general, across our planet, the more hospitable the climate, the more diversity we see. Tropical regions are typically richly diverse, whereas polar regions support fewer species. In much the same way, we encounter workplaces that seem warm and welcoming to diversity, and others that are cold to it.

So Fast You Don't Know What Hit You

Rapid environmental changes typically cause mass extinctions. One estimate is that less than 1 percent of the species that originally existed on Earth are still present on it.

Since life on Earth began, five major mass extinctions—as well as several minor ones—have led to sudden drops in the number of our planet's species. Unfortunately, since the emergence of humans, the reduction in biodiversity has been dramatic, with an accompanying loss of genetic diversity. Named the Holocene extinction, this reduction is thought to be primarily caused by the proliferation of humans impacting and destroying habitats, or climate change, or both.

We humans, to a great extent, are very much in control of our immediate environments, much more so than any other species on the planet. We don't, for example, have to let "extinction" happen in our professional environments. Rather, we can design them to accommodate diversity. At the same time, we must remember that our primitive brains know nothing of long-term strategic thinking, and will therefore be completely opposed to the idea of connecting with other humans who are different from ourselves.

This is why we have to make a conscious effort to support diversity; without it, the workplace will come to resemble a hall of mirrors, and sound like an echo chamber, producing only a limited set of ideas about what to do when trouble comes.

Species Depend on Each Other

The validity of the theory of survival of the fittest within any given species cannot be denied, yet each species depends on the "services" provided by other species for its survival. This type of cooperation, based on mutual survival, is often termed the *balanced ecosystem*.

Why is it then that businesspeople often ask, "How can we clone it?," which is a short-term measure with long-term disadvantages. Cloning is how the simplest organisms on the planet—like bacteria—reproduce. They do it quickly, multiplying in the millions. But when a strong dose of penicillin comes their way, they are reliant on a chance mutation to immunize themselves against their annihilation. Unlike us humans, they can't hold a meeting and come up with new ways to address the situation.

Let's look at what we do need at a primitive level to create and manage a thriving diverse system: a tribe that will survive and reach its goals by moving forward—not standing still.

The Tribal Environment

As we know, tribes are a result of their environment. They may establish and follow rules as a direct response to the behavior needed to be best fit for their environment—today. Or, they may react to a characteristic of the tribe's origins, such as where it came from (in time or space) and the behaviors that were needed in the past to accommodate that environment.

For example, while we may recognize that many old customs and traditions seem out of sync with modern life, we can understand how and why they developed when we consider the context in which they originated. Some religious tribes adhere to laws that dictate what not to eat, and define what is "unclean," rules that, in a modern-day supermarket, have no relation to literal cleanliness or being dangerous to ingest. Yet some of these laws were both sensible and essential when we consider their origins in the nomadic desert culture of thousands of years ago—regardless of what the religion

(continued)

(*continued*)

may have stated as the *spiritual* or *theistic* reasoning behind such laws.

Similarly, in the workplace, customary or traditional ways of behaving can seem old-fashioned to a newer member of the group. For example, it's often a necessity for an entrepreneurial tribe to work 24/7 in order to build a company. But after the company is built, and is stable and successful, newer members may not see the need to continue that behavior. The baby boomer owner who built the organization might still be found at her desk at 7:30 PM on a Friday evening, because her limbic brain is programmed through her experiences to believe in the dictum that "If you don't work hard, and keeping working hard, everything will be lost." Yet many of her gen-Y or millennial employees will have left the office after lunch to pursue a long weekend of downtime activities, because their limbic brains and their experience tells them they can trust that the company will still be there on Monday morning. They have spent their formative years working at large companies that are as rooted in the corporate landscape as 100-year-old oak trees. They have no knowledge that only a few saplings make it to maturation every five years or so—unlike the boomer founder, who is trying to get one of her seedlings to grow into an oak and does not want to leave it even for a second, lest a deer come and eat it.

Neither of these generations will probably ever convince the other that its reality is the true one. Indeed, they may come to verbal blows over it, with the owner demanding from her employees a work ethic more consistent with her own, and the employees using their power-in-numbers to maintain their holding pattern.

I was recently interviewed by a potential client who had been relocated from Korea to run the North

American arm of his multinational firm. He wanted to undergo communication training that would help him persuade his employees to work according to his expectations of them. I suggested to him that although communication training would improve his ability to convey his perspective to his North American employees, his core message, to "behave more like my Korean staff," would not resonate. From my point of view, what he really needed help with was dealing with the disappointment and disdain he felt for his North American colleagues. His company needed the business in North America, and needed a North American workforce to action it. He had to face that he was in their territory and among their tribe, and so would have to work very hard to learn to deal with their very different values and belief systems about work if he wished to lead them successfully.

To put all this in perspective for him, I said, "The people here have been working on how to behave in order to live well in this land for a long, long time. Your company has been around for a number of decades. And you, personally, may have moved on in three years' time. Who—or what—has the real power here? And what are you going to do about that?" He decided he wanted help with this; however, he required his training syllabus to be laid out in an orderly manner, and to have a timetable to which he and I would strictly adhere. Even after he had accepted at an intellectual level that he had to adapt his personal tribal mentality, his primitive limbic brain still wanted that change delivered in the way comfortable to him.

As I pointed to in the opening story to this chapter, the primitive brain does not recognize irony.

Environmental Conditions for a Great Team

Every organizational system needs clear boundaries, a defined territory within which it works. Otherwise, it will overextend its reach and run out of energy. Job descriptions, work schedules, budgets, goals, and objectives are all forms of boundaries.

Within these boundaries, there has to be a level of interdependence among the members of the team. Whether they are individualists or collectivists (as discussed in Chapter Eighteen), they need to need each other and be related in some way. Otherwise, they will treat each other as nothing more than drains on their personal energy stores. Each must look to be of service to the others in order to better everyone's existence.

Great teams also require a social structure within which to carry out their collective work. Knowing who the decision maker is, that it is someone they can confide in with complete confidence, and with whom they can share a joke, frees up energy for the task at hand. Without social structure, our primitive brain has to expend energy constantly in an effort to determine where we stand in the group. Basic rules or core norms of conduct enable team members to work together consistently toward their goals under a variety of conditions.

On top of this, a level of stability within the membership over time is essential, to establish a sense of certainty and predictability. The team also needs a compelling direction or a goal, a clear, challenging common purpose that is of consequence to their well-being, and the well-being of their other ecosystems and the other tribes therein. The primitive brain focuses on the "end," whereas the modern brain focuses on the "means." In today's complex world, we need the tactical and strategic capabilities of the neocortex to win the day. Unless our goal is clear, and we regard it as desirable, the primitive brain will not give up control to the neocortex, nor allow it to spend time imagining, planning, co-opting others into that plan, and executing.

Most importantly, the team needs shared values. Imagine the problems when one person values quality while another places a higher value on frugality. Or, half the team values time with family, and leaves at 4:00 PM every Friday, while the other half values "getting their bonuses," and so chooses to work nights and weekends. In good times, these differences won't matter; but they can sound the death knell to team spirit when it's crunch time, at the end of a tough quarter.

Leading Teams Well

Given all of this, the leader's main responsibility is to ensure that the environment is optimal for the team. She must make sure that the team's basic performance conditions are sound, and then help members take the greatest possible advantage of their favorable circumstances.

Leadership at this level involves deciding on, and then competently executing, those actions that are most likely to create and sustain the conditions just identified. Anyone who helps do that, including individual team members who hold no formal leadership role, could be said to be exercising leadership.

Effective leaders must, therefore, be aware of the conditions that most powerfully support team effectiveness. They need to be able to extract and/or highlight, from situations, those factors that are most consequential for high performance levels. They then must use this information to narrow the gap between the team's present performance and what that team could—and *should*—be achieving.

Leading a team can be an emotionally challenging undertaking, especially when it comes to managing both one's own anxiety and that of others in the environment. Recall that it is the nature of our primitive brain to move away from anxiety-arousing states. As a leader, you may need to engage your neocortex to be curious about unstable environments. This may well be the only way to learn more about the nature of such situations, and thereby arrange, or rearrange, the factors to ensure your tribe's survival and success.

Leadership involves moving a system from where it is now to some other, *better* place. That means the leader must operate at the *margins*, where team members are comfortable and prefer to be, rather than at the *center* of the consensus. This may force the leader to defy existing group norms and disrupt established routines. By doing so, she may encounter anger and resistance, stirred up by both the team members' limbic systems and their reptilian brains. But it is only those leaders who are courageous enough to confront the tribe's norms who will be able to make significant transformations in the way their teams operate.

Day Twenty Action

What level of diversity in the workplace environment does your team or tribe need to reach its goals? What constrains your team to remain the same?

Does your team have a clear and solid goal? What are the team's shared values? Are they clear to all, or do they seem variable to some? What about boundaries: Do they shift? Interdependence and stability: Is it firm or shaky? How would you describe the social structure of the team: Does it suit the variety of people involved in the mission?

Manage Primitive Impulses Now
Feng Shui for the Mind

When the team isn't working as you had hoped, rather than telling them to "work better," and putting more pressure on them, which ultimately can cause them to take flight, or fight, look for the cause of the dysfunction in their environment. Then try and create something different there: Introduce greater diversity, and watch what grows. Remember the words of the great World War II leader, Sir Winston Churchill: "We shape our buildings; thereafter, they shape us." Why not reshape the building in which you work to get the best out of yourself and others, instead of trying to constantly manage your impulsive reactions to it? And if you can't reshape the office, consider holding team meetings in different places: in a coffee shop, in the parking lot on a sunny day, at a country retreat, or on the rooftop, to give you a high-level view of the project. Who knows what introducing a more diverse outlook could bring?

Day 21

Changing Tribes Is Expensive
Neuroplasticity and the Limbic Brain

When the facts change, I change my mind. What do you do, sir?

—John Maynard Keynes

Today you'll tame:
◆ Your constant friend and mine: change!

She was senior officer at a financial organization, and highly regarded externally; she was regularly featured in magazines and appeared often on business news channels.

But when the new CEO arrived from the parent company, he began to leave her out of major decisions, making it crystal clear to her that, for whatever reason, there was no longer a place in the company for her.

She spent her energy complaining to colleagues, coaches, and family; talked about leaving; and came up with exit strategies. Yet she never pulled the trigger. Just the opposite; she did everything she could to convince herself that she needed to stay: "The project needs me." "My team needs me." "We need to get through performance and compensation review season." And even, "I need to stand on the ship as it sinks!"

She had one foot on the gas and another on the brake. Her engine made a powerful noise, but she went nowhere. She was paralyzed in the face of change.

By the time all her projects had been cancelled, all her team had either resigned or been axed. Finally, she was let go—led abruptly and ungraciously from the building by security, carrying a box of her belongings. To date, she still had never managed to work out how to tell the CEO she was resigning.

Why did the dinosaurs become extinct?

There are numerous theories as to what initiated the unsupportive environment that caused the Cretaceous–Paleogene extinction event 65 million years ago, which led to the demise of the "great lizards." Given that about 90 percent of the dinosaurs are known to have been plant eaters, one of the theories (introduced in Chapter Three) is that an asteroid hit Earth, throwing countless tons of dust into the atmosphere and blocking the sunlight. The result was a "long night," which led to a dearth of food for the dinosaurs. Without reliable food sources, compounded by a series of other catastrophes, the dinosaurs became extinct.

One thing is certain: they're gone. The entire shift seems to have taken no more than 10,000 years to complete. Though this may sound like forever to us, it's a moment in time in the grand scheme of evolution—yet long enough for any species able to adapt quickly to the new environment to secure a niche within it.

The problem was that the dinosaurs were *not* able to adapt to their new surroundings. The environmental change was too expensive for these enormous creatures; and in the end, their inability to "invest" forced them to pay the ultimate price—being ignored by kids in museums who would rather be playing Angry Birds on their computers.

How do we extricate ourselves from environments that we realize are doing us harm, especially those that feel so much like home to us?

The One Constant

Change is always personal.

As I've said throughout the book, our primitive brain *hates* change. It interprets constancy and familiarity as predictability, which gives us a better chance of survival. Change brings uncertainty and confusion, and I have yet to meet a human being who claims to enjoy being confused.

Leaving a company—or a profession, for that matter—is a huge change. It is no wonder that so many people (like the woman we met at the beginning of chapter) refuse to leave—until they are forced out, or the company goes under.

When you consider that the workplace provides much of our social structure, and that our coworkers form our tribe, the notion of leaving voluntarily becomes even more difficult and frightening.

Leaving the Tribe

Different people leave in different ways. Some walk out. Some get kicked out. Some just burn out. Others grow out. Others find out or get counseled out.

The walkouts tend to rebel from the situation and resign. Or in more extreme cases of rebellion, they simply never show up at work again, adopting the attitude that since they couldn't measure up to the system's requirements—the values, beliefs, rituals, customs, goals, concerns, or signals—there isn't a place for them in that tribe, so they might as well take off. Understandably, this may leave them with feelings of inadequacy and, often, animosity toward the rest of the tribe. Some, in an attempt to avoid those feelings, may, instead of walking out, opt (usually unconsciously) to feel the pain of trying to fit in rather than the pain of dropping out. Those who get kicked out—excommunicated, shunned, or fired—also usually have failed to adhere to the tribal norms of behavior, in one way or another. They may then be filled with grief and guilt, yet still feel loyal to the group that rejected them.

Burnouts are the people have been so drained by the tribe—spiritually, mentally, physically, emotionally, and/or financially—they cease to be able to function on a normal basis anymore. Some burnouts may even exhibit symptoms of post-traumatic stress disorder (PTSD), commonly experienced by war survivors; they are usually very confused, perhaps even physically ill, terrified generally, and unable to trust anyone—most of all themselves.

The findouts are those who are given, counseled to realize, or stumble onto, data that causes them to no longer align with the tribe's behavioral norms. Other tribe members might perceive them as whistleblowers or turncoats.

Roger That!

Beliefs, like values, can be very hard to change—barring a catastrophic event that forces the change. But they can also change over time, and with the new tribe's support.

(continued)

(continued)

Like our values, we can categorize our beliefs, into two different types: *empowering* and *limiting*. Empowering beliefs help us to take on and live within our environment confidently. Empowering beliefs enable us to make sound decisions in what can often be an ambiguous world. Limiting beliefs do the exact opposite; they keep us rooted in particular positions within our environment that ultimately bar us from reaching some of our desires or potential. Typically, a number of our limiting beliefs are based on assumptions that turn out not to be true.

The way the brain processes the environment in relation to our values and beliefs is what leads us to make both our unconscious and conscious decisions, and essentially controls our behavior; this is similar to the way a computer's hardware and software work together to control its outputs.

Human decision-making is a largely unconscious process by which a constantly shifting hierarchy of internalized values interacts with a constantly shifting set of perceived circumstances and retrieved memories. In other words, our brain is the hardware of our behavioral control system. Decision-making begins when our senses present information to our brain about our current situation. But as we know, our primitive limbic system also has access to memories of other situations and decisions, as well as previously acquired knowledge and perspectives. At the heart of this process is our hierarchy of internalized values. Our limbic brain takes these informational elements and arrives at a response to the situation—a decision to act in a particular way, or to not act at all.

Roger Sperry, who won a Nobel Prize for his split-brain research, put it this way:

In addition to their commonly recognized significance from a personal, religious, or philosophic standpoint, [human values] can also be viewed objectively as universal determinants in all human decision making. All decisions boil down to a choice among alternatives of what is most valued, for whatever reasons, and are determined by the particular value system that prevails. Human value priorities, viewed thus in objective control-system theory, stand out as the most strategically powerful causal control now shaping world events. More than any other causal system with which science now concerns itself, it is variables in human value systems that will determine the future.

Well put, Roger.

There are times when your relationship with the tribe is not going well, until eventually you have to admit that things aren't going to work out. Keeping in mind that breakups (personal or professional) almost always occur in four stages, knowing which stage you are at can help you to deal with the upheaval a little better. It also helps to keep in mind that just about everyone has been through this process at some point in their life and has come through—and sometimes are the better for it. This alone should give you hope for better workdays ahead.

Here are the four stages of a professional breakup:

1. **Shock.** For some, this can be the most emotional and gut-wrenching stage of the whole ordeal. Most of us are taken by surprise at this stage—remember, our primitive brain hates surprise—and we can act impulsively. If you don't handle this part of the leaving process correctly, you can cause permanent damage—completely kill any chance of reconciliation down the road.

2. **Denial.** After the initial shock is over, you may convince yourself that the breakup was nothing more than a minor disagreement, and the tribe will come around eventually. Unfortunately, you are likely continuing to communicate with the group, thereby adding fuel to the fire.

3. **Depression.** Once you acknowledge that you are leaving the company for real, and are about to be on your own, depression can set in fairly quickly. Often, you spend days reminiscing and obsessing about the people you used to hang out with and the work you were doing—thereby putting your search for new work on the back burner.

4. **Acceptance.** It's at this stage that you come to terms with the breakup and convince yourself that it's *really over*. You should be over the initial grief at this point; however, you may still feel incredibly sad over the fact that you truly must move on, find a new group, and lead a new life. You're forced to accept that it simply wasn't meant to be, and that you have to start rebuilding your work life and looking for a new team to join.

◆ At some point in our lives we all have to leave the tribe in order to discard obsolete ways of being, thinking, and feeling. This doesn't mean, necessarily, that we have to turn our back on all the key influences on our development? Many of us identify ourselves powerfully as distinct individuals; therefore, we may not realize the depth of the tribe's imprint on our psyche. But it does—subliminally yet significantly—direct and shape our lives. To leave the tribe, we must relinquish our attachment to the security of the "group-think." But forfeiting the comfort zone causes pain for the brain; gone are: Certainty about how to think and respond. In the old tribe, this was "inexpensive" for the brain.

♦ Approval from others: This felt good to the brain and encouraged it to keep on having inexpensive thoughts and taking inexpensive actions.

♦ The safety net of the tribe: During those times you may have been original/innovative; both of which are risky, and come at a high price taking energy to imagine all the potential outcomes.

♦ Your certainty of your position within the hierarchy: In a new tribe, starting over carries risk—one wrong step and you could be thrown out.

Beware! It feels very dangerous to the limbic, social primitive brain to leave the tribe! This is because early in evolution, our survival was possible only within a tribal context. Threatened by independent thought, traditional linkages discourage genius and its innate inclination toward unregimented attitudes, imagination, and creativity. Our natural loyalty to the family, community, or greater society, which has given us life, context, support, nourishment, safety, and connection, compels us to honor those who have paved the way. We've gotten to where we are thanks to their accomplishments and authority, and their ongoing influence can reduce our learning curve over time.

Long after we have gone, we will carry the tribe with us in our head. And silencing their voices may be the biggest challenge of all.

Day Twenty-One Action

Think about how many tribes you have moved on from in your life. Which ones hurt the most to leave, and why? Which ones did you make the best transition out of or into, and why do you think these shifts were so smooth?

Manage Primitive Impulses Now
New Kid on the Block

Many of us find it hard to begin a new job. As a new employer or colleague, you may find that the person you interviewed, and who seemed likely to fit in smoothly, turns out to be a non-matching piece in the corporate jigsaw puzzle, after he actually joins the group.

You can help new employees understand the group's values, beliefs, goals, and concerns by asking what their approach might be to these, rather than stand by and watch them make huge behavioral mistakes and faux pas. For example, when the group has to attend a regular event or fulfill a particular duty or a tradition, make sure the new people receive an invite (since they won't know to attend on an instinctual level, like others do). Make sure they also know what kinds of things to expect, and what the normal behaviors are (about which, again, they won't have an instinct; they are not mind readers.) Assigning them a "buddy" or a mentor is another great way to help new recruits navigate the maze of written and unwritten rules that every workplace has.

Week IV

New You
Higher Planes

The mind is like a parachute—it works only when it's open.
—Frank Zappa

The newest, most recently developed and evolved part of your brain makes up about 2 percent of your total body weight but uses the vast majority of the 20 percent of your body's energy that goes into entire brain function—enough to power a light bulb. It is this newest part of your brain that you use for voluntary movement, forward thinking, logic, imagination, creativity, abstraction, problem solving, language, Sudoku, and a bunch of other time-consuming but totally cool activities.

This part of the brain is, however, a costly piece of equipment to carry around with you, especially when you are in a stressful situation and would like to lighten your load. Just reading this page will cost your body a quarter of your lung capacity for oxygen. (Let's hope it finds it worth the expense!) No wonder the primitive brain wants to shut down critical thinking capacity when the body is under stress. The intelligent and imaginative mind is a force to be reckoned with, but what with the cost of running it we often use it less frequently than we would like.

Keeping "your head when all about you are losing theirs," as Rudyard Kipling suggested, is an expensive proposition. You can, however, optimize your ability to keep a wise head on your shoulders under stress by mindfully creating and constructing an environment within which you, as well as those with whom you work, are better able to think more rationally, intelligently, and creatively. This is an optimal environment for countering the more primitive reactions that we tend to fall back on in times of crisis.

In the final part of the book we are going to reexamine what your behavior looks like under pressure, and how you can help others monitor theirs when the $@#! hits the fan. By helping your brain to respond in new ways to some very old signals, we can form a new "you," when it comes to dealing with your own impulsive behaviors and those of others; a new you that can use your mind in the most highly evolved manner, even in extreme circumstances.

We'll start this process by considering the mind of Socrates, as described by Plato: "The only true wisdom is in knowing you know nothing."

Day 22

Suspend Judgment
Put It to One Side

I used to think anyone doing anything weird was weird. Now I know that it is the people that call others weird that are weird.
—Paul McCartney

Today you'll tame:
- Your old viewpoint

When the new associate joined the company he was immediately asked to put a bid in on a new project that could fall right into the company's sweet spot—$200K. But when he looked at the specs from the client, he assessed its value at 10 times that amount.

His boss's instinctive response to being told that was cut and dried: "You're crazy. We'll never get it; we don't do jobs that big. Scale it back to the minimum or we'll lose the job."

The new associate, who had come from a firm that was familiar with working on projects "this big," tried to make it clear to his new boss that he understood it was

(continued)

(continued)

out of the company's usual scope, but that he was quite comfortable working on projects of this magnitude. He added that he had the experience, albeit at a junior level.

The boss was calmed by his new hire's assurances, and so suspended his judgment about the company's ability to win this project. He assigned the associate to submit the higher bid on the contract.

The company won the job.

As you well understand by now, we pass judgment on everyone and everything, whether we mean to or not. And we base every assessment we make about someone else's behavior (why they do what they do) on a theory we have; that is, we can't make a judgment without some criteria or a model that makes sense to us, whether consciously or unconsciously.

Even when we assure ourselves, "I am not making a judgment," we are. Saying we are not just reflects that we are not conscious of doing it, nor of the theory upon which we are basing the judgment. This is dangerous, or at the very least ignorant.

How's that for passing judgment?!

It is far better to acknowledge that we judge, even when we think we don't, than to assume we are not, when in fact we are. Simply put, we cannot stop ourselves from making judgments all the time (good weather/bad weather; good food/bad food; nice outfit/you look like $%^# in that!) any more than we can stop ourselves from breathing. Both are instinctual and hardwired into our primitive brain.

What we can do is try to *suspend* our judgment temporarily. This means first acknowledging that we have made the judgment, and then choosing to put it to one side for a moment or two. Doing so gives us an opportunity to gather more and different data about the situation, so that we can judge it again in a more open-minded way. Yes, we may arrive at the same judgment, if it is supported by the new information we gathered. On the other hand, we may learn something new that fundamentally changes our assessment of the situation.

The Doctor Is In

Our primitive brain is always quickly diagnosing everything we come into contact with, and sense. And by "diagnosing," I mean "getting to know" by deconstructing the parts. However, the way our primitive brain deconstructs its environment and the events that happen within it can take into account only our limited life experiences. Imagine, for example, how differently you might feel about a tumor in the cerebellum of your brain than a world-class neurosurgeon would. What you may interpret as a possible death sentence, the surgeon views as a potentially curable illness. Your emotional response is, understandably, fear, whereas the surgeon's might be excitement, about the challenge she is presented with. You may see no future except death, whereas she can imagine many possible, and positive, scenarios for the outcome. The point is, our personal theories—the way we evaluate people and situations—influence the judgments we make about them, and ultimately dictate what we believe to be true.

In short: *The behavior of everything around us is a result of our viewpoint.*

Let's break that statement down and dig into it with all we know so far:

◆ You judge everything.
◆ The diagnosis that leads to your judgments is the result of a theory you hold, consciously or unconsciously.
◆ Some theories you inherit and some are derived from your life experiences.

- If you believe you don't have a theory, you are working from a theory about which you are unconscious.
- Your theories have gotten you this far in life, so good for them.
- Some of your theories have been, or could, in the future, be limiting.
- People's theories (points of view) can differ subtly or radically.
- All theories influence behavior.
- In certain environments, even a subtle difference in theories can cause extreme variations in behavior.

Here's the biggest kicker:
- Differences (even small ones) in behavior often lead to conflict.

The big question here is: "How can we change our viewpoint so that our resulting behavior does not cause conflict?"

The answer is: "Maybe we can't!"

What we can do is to put our viewpoint to one side for a moment; suspend our initial judgment to give us time to explore and experience other viewpoints to see whether it is possible to form a new and different viewpoint.

How do we suspend judgment?

Fuel for Thought

One of my first jobs was in a garage—pumping gas and manning the cash register. Early on, the manager, a guy called Kit, said something quite important and useful for me, as a teenager, to hear. He began with, "This job will teach you about life, Mark."

I thought I was about to get a typical postwar lecture on the value of hard work, saving money, and understanding our place in the world. I was wrong. What he then said was: "You'll learn that you can't judge people by how they initially look. Everyone comes here. You are going to see them all: the guy driving the Porsche, the gypsy travelers towing their caravan, the lady in her fur coat and Rolls, the commercial goods vehicle driver, the boy racer, and the driver of the family hatchback."

His concluding remark was, "Be on the QT," British Air Force shorthand for "Be quiet and observe."

He was right. Everyone did come in to the garage. I found that many surprised me, in some way, as long as I kept my judgments to myself and opened my eyes to what was *really* going on.

STEP ONE: MAKE IT A GOAL

Setting goals and objectives is a tried-and-true way to start doing something difficult. Whether the goal is huge, like competing in the Olympics, or smaller, like losing a couple of pounds, achieving it begins by setting it. Many successful businesspeople will tell you they set goals for themselves, and then set off on the journey to reach them, a journey made up of many small steps, some forward and some backward, but all taken while keeping an eye on the prize.

The goal here is to *suspend judgment*—not to stop making judgments or be less judgmental.

STEP TWO: PRACTICE BEING DESCRIPTIVE RATHER THAN JUDGMENTAL

Don't say: "Yours is a weak argument!" Say instead: "Your point of view hasn't convinced me." In this case, you are not judging the other's viewpoint; you are describing your internal thinking about her viewpoint.

To practice means to do something over and over, and regularly. If you are at all like me, when you begin to practice anything, you will do it poorly, or not at all. We have all heard that "practice makes perfect," which, from my experience, may not be a universally correct statement; but to reach the goal of suspending judgment, if you persevere, and work at being *descriptive*, I'm confident you will improve in this effort.

Still, not all practice leads to improvement. It's not uncommon for many of us to continue to make the same mistakes over and over. That's why practice *with feedback* is essential to our improvement. Feedback does not necessarily mean having someone inform you as to how you did. If you practice your golf swing at the driving range, you get feedback just by watching to see how far out, and in what direction, the ball goes.

How do we get feedback when we are attempting to suspend our judgment, to be more "descriptive"? My experience is that when I make a judgment about someone, particularly a negative one, the conversation between us stops; perhaps the other becomes defensive. In contrast, when I am being descriptive and totally neutral in terms of any judgment, the conversation continues to progress.

Being descriptive means, simply, using words to describe the situation, itself, rather than the *meaning* of the situation (which is where the expression of your judgments comes in). For example, there is a big difference between, "You spilled coffee all over my report. Why can't you be more careful?" and "Hey, there is a brown stain on this report." The former will likely lead to defensiveness, whereas the latter will often lead to an apology from the person who spilled the coffee.

Step Three: Pretend You Have No Judgment

We've all heard the adage, "Fake it 'till you make it." What this means is that if you behave in a certain way, even if you aren't thinking that way and feeling that way, over time you will lay down new neural pathways that support the behavior. When these new connections become strong and lasting, through repeated stimulation, the new behavior will become "second nature."

So while you are practicing being more descriptive, and failing miserably, keep your judgments to yourself. Others will try and get you to verbalize your judgments, convinced that you have them (and they are right). When asked outright, "What do think about Suresh's idea?" saying you have no judgment about it will be interpreted as "I'm not sure." Yes, it may be a lie; inside you may be screaming, "It's the dumbest idea I have ever heard!" But it's a lie in support of a good cause: improving your ability to learn more about ideas before judging them.

What about authenticity, you might ask. Isn't that one of the success factors in the workplace, and relationships in general? Yes; and people can often tell when you are being inauthentic. But in this case, you are authentically working to improve a skill: suspending judgment. It's just that you may not be doing it very well yet, and so it doesn't come across as authentic. If confronted about this, you might say, "I'm working on suspending judgments. It's just not that easy to do." How is that for authenticity?

Besides, isn't it your authentic primitive self that gets you into trouble time and again—making judgments about this and that, and running roughshod over other people's points of view? Being less authentic now and again may even help some of your professional relationships, rather than hinder them.

Act Up

Need more help in your effort to suspend judgment? Try this: Imagine what you might do while you are suspending judgment. Maybe you wait to hear out in its entirety what someone has to say before expressing your thoughts. Or perhaps you breathe in slowly and evenly while you listen to her or watch her behavior.

Whatever personal course of action you decide on to help you act as if you are suspending judgment, might just help you fall naturally into actually suspending your judgment.

Day Twenty-Two Action

It's pointless to say "don't judge," because you will. There is a lot to be gained, however, from suspending your judgments even as you make them, if only for a moment. After all, you can always go back to your original assessment, if all that you discover doesn't change your mind!

Practice today suspending your judgments. Here's how:

1. Notice when you've made, or are in the process of making, a judgment, and make a point to suspend it.
2. Put the judgment to one side by saying to yourself, "Okay, that's my initial judgment; now what else might I consider?" Then describe to yourself what else is involved in the situation.
3. List some actions you can take when you are trying to be less judgmental, and more open. Now try taking those actions. For example, when I am suspending my judgment, I open my eyes a little wider, tilt my head to one side to listen more attentively, and I let others speak until they are through, before I say my piece.

Manage Primitive Impulses Now
What a Performance!

In the workplace, we are frequently asked for our judgments. And no situation is more fraught with risk of expressing them than at our annual performance review. All employees dread them, and managers sweat over them. If this is part of your job description, there is no better place to practice being descriptive and pretending that you have no judgments.

Day 23

Be Curious

Recognize People

The real voyage of discovery consists not in seeking new landscapes but in having new eyes.

—Marcel Proust

Today you'll tame:
◆ Your primitive outlook

Seth, one of the trainees, had been "loudly quiet" all day—apart from a number sharply pointed, negative comments he made about the training materials, which spun off into a diatribe of discontent about the ever-increasing workloads the company expected him to carry.

Three-quarters of the way through the morning, Seth suddenly stood up and approached the whiteboard in a quite aggressive manner. His face red, he hovered menacingly at the front of the class while leaning toward the content on the board.

The training facilitator refrained from assuming that Seth was going blow his top. Instead, he asked Seth,

(continued)

(continued)

"I notice you have moved in closer. What is going on for you?"

"This is great stuff!" Seth effused to the whole group. "We all need to pay attention to this. It can really help us."

For the rest of the session, Seth actively supported the content the trainer was delivering, and even helped others to understand it by the comments he made.

As we discussed in the previous chapter, every examination we make of anything or anyone is based on and contextualized within a theory we hold; that theory is our viewpoint. So every time we see someone we work with, we are seeing him from our viewpoint—not his own or anyone else's. But when we look again, through new eyes—say, for example, from our coworker's viewpoint—we stand a chance of interpreting it differently. This may mean we are becoming enlightened; we see something we missed previously, or failed to understand.

Read that word again: "enlightened." It means to shine light on something so that we can see it more clearly. How can we illuminate the world around us, so that we can pick out fresh details?

Ask Questions

One of the simplest and most effective ways of discovering a new perspective is to be curious, and indulge that curiosity by asking questions. This uses your neocortex and effectively suspends your primitive brain's best-fit thinking for a bit. But if you don't suspend your judgment, you won't be curious enough to ask any questions, because you will have already made up your mind about the issue or person.

To encourage your curiosity, here are the types of questions that Socrates, one of the founders of modern thinking, recommended:

- **Clarification questions:** How many people will be attending? What is the cost of training for the new software? How long has the company been in existence?

    Clarification questions provide the missing pieces and thus fill in the picture. They give us more specific information about the issue, product, service, and people.

    You can always use the basic catch-all query: "Can you tell me more?" to jump-start for everyone the process of going deeper into the pool of data available.

- **Assumption questions:** Is anything we are discussing based on an assumption? What could we assume instead? How can we verify or disprove our assumptions?

    Probing at assumptions helps everyone reassess their unproven beliefs, theories, or viewpoints. The answers you get or those you yourself come up with, can shake loose the bedrock attached to the unproductive ways of looking at a person or issue.

- **Reason or evidence questions:** Why are we having this discussion? What would be an example of that? Do you have any proof? What could be causing all of this?

    When you can uncover the rationale behind a behavior, often you can find good evidence for it. If the evidence is not there, it may indicate you should go back and question your assumptions again. To build your business or organization on solid ground, you need solid reasons and evidence for doing so.

- **Viewpoint and perspective questions:** Is there an alternate way to look at this? Have you looked at it from another's point of view? What might be the bigger picture here? How do you feel about this? What are your thoughts?

  Some call this *perceptual positioning*. Taking into consideration that in any situation there is the way that you, yourself, see it, the way others see it, and the way a spectator might see it, can help uncover a formerly hidden view of the picture. A new view opens the mind to new theories and new judgments, and potentially new realities about the situation.

- **Implications and consequences questions:** What are the consequences of this action? How will it affect you? How do you think it will affect me? What might happen if we take no action, instead?

  Understanding people's judgments about the effect an action might have on them or on you can often enlighten you as to why they are doing what they are doing. Otherwise, all you have are your own ideas about the outcome, available or desired. Needless to say, you also can, and probably should, question your own evaluation of the outcomes.

- **Questions about the questions:** Am I making sense when I ask these questions? Is there a question that I should ask you regarding this issue? Is asking questions about this issue the most useful way to move forward, today? Am I asking the right people?

  This process can be infuriatingly complicated, but worth the trouble, as it can help you expand your narrow view of the world, by inviting a critique of your line of investigation, which has led to the judgments you have made. No one is infallible, not even Socrates, so why not question these Socratic questions themselves?

The reptilian brain, unfortunately, is only interested in clarification questions, because they tend to be simple (When is the meeting?), immediate (What are we having for lunch?), or tactical (What are we pricing the new product at?)

As you know, the reptilian brain is totally self-centered, so it will never be interested in other peoples' viewpoints (or their thoughts and feelings), and it will never question its assumptions (beliefs without evidence to support them). In order to be able to ask questions, you need to be able to manage your reptilian brain. Not easy to do when you are tired, rushed, threatened or stressed out.

The limbic system, the relational and emotional center of our brain, *is* interested in points of view presented by other members of your tribe, though not necessarily by those of people from different tribes. And, of course, because it is tribal, the limbic system will pay particular attention to points of view proposed by those higher in rank than you, and probably ignore those who are lower in rank.

It's our neocortex that gives us the ability to ask all six types of questions. Easy to engage when we are calm and relaxed. Not so easy at other times.

If you notice you are having difficulty engaging your modern, inquisitive brain at any given moment, it might indicate it's time to say, "Let's come back to this tomorrow." Do what every kindergarten teacher knows to do in times of stress: take a timeout.

Standing Their Ground

It is fair to say that most arguments are presented from a particular position. Even those who say they represent no point of view have taken *that* up as their position. So reassessing a viewpoint by questioning others' positions and, most importantly, your own, can lead to better management of your instinctive and impulsive behaviors. It also allows others to see how their actions might be the result of a one-sided view of the situation.

Let Me Meditate on It

A good friend and one-time student of mine, Toni Grates, started a yoga studio, with a partner, at the same time she became pregnant with her first child, *and* "inherited" two bonus children from her recent marriage. Thirteen manic months later, her business partner had left, and her yoga business collapsed in an epic fashion. Still, Toni managed to stay relatively sane and keep her relationship with her husband and family intact.

She now writes a great blog about it all, called namastebitchesblog.com. Read this excerpt from it, and think about it, as we'll discuss it later in this chapter.

> *Coming up with a name for our [yoga] studio was fairly challenging. Sanskrit words were out, as were all words synonymous with breathing. Yoga poses were also out, as was anything involving the words "energy," "om," "lotus," or "chakra." "Toni Grates' Yoga Emporium" seemed like a mouthful, and "Real Deal Yoga" left me tongue-tied, so we decided to keep it simple and name the studio after our geographical location.*
>
> *And Village Yoga Canada was born.*
>
> *It was only a matter of weeks before we received a letter from Diane, the owner and founder of Village Yoga on the Jersey shore.*
>
> *Dear Village Yoga Canada,*
>
> *I recently received an e-mail from one of your members thinking that we were you, which we're not, because we're us. We are Village Yoga, serving the*

residents of the Jersey Shore. You need to change your name, because this is going to get very confusing for our members, and that's not cool. We had the name first and I don't want my members getting confused.

I'm hoping you're going to be ethical about this.

Namaste,

Diane

Unsure as to how anyone could confuse "Village Yoga Canada" with "Village Yoga on the Jersey Shore," I e-mailed her back.

Dear Diane,

Thanks for your e-mail. I'm sorry that you received an e-mail from one of our members in error. We assure you that we're not out to take members from you, especially since you're 9–10 hours away from us. We've named our studio after our geographical location, and I would assume that your members will know we're not you since the word "Canada" is a part of our name.

We're happy to talk with you on the phone about this. It is not our intention to be unethical about anything.

Thanks for your time,

Village Yoga Canada

I didn't hear back from Diane for about 2 months.

(continued)

(continued)

Dear Village Yoga Canada,

I got another 4 e-mails from your members asking me questions about your schedule. Clearly, I don't have time for this and it's getting in the way of the work I need to do at my studio.

I have no other option but to take legal action if you don't immediately change your name. I had Village Yoga first and it's mine.

Namaste,

Diane from VILLAGE YOGA

At this point, for solely my own entertainment, I started imagining that Diane was Snookie from the hit reality show Jersey Shore *and that all her members were foul-mouthed Jersey Shore brats, who went to yoga to pick up.*

Diane,

We're not changing our name since we've legally been advised that it is available in Canada, and since there is really no way that your members could possibly confuse "Village Yoga on the Jersey Shore" with "Village Yoga Canada."

We're sorry that our members have again contacted you. Since our e-mail addresses are fairly similar, we will figure out a new address to go by.

This is yoga, right? So there's no need for lawsuits.

Thanks for understanding,

Village Yoga CANADA

> *Village Yoga Canada,*
>
> *I have a log of 13 people who have contacted us think-*
> *ing we are you. I used to work in NYC and I know a*
> *LOT of good lawyers. You will be hearing from one of*
> *them VERY soon, since you insist on being unethical.*
> *I have no choice but to sue you for damages.*
>
> *Namaste,*
>
> *Village Yoga on the Jersey Shore*
>
> *I never did hear from Diane's lawyer. I'm assuming*
> *it's because she looked at a map and realized that*
> *the Jersey Shore is nowhere near Toronto, Canada.*
> *Or maybe she took the time to reflect on the wise and*
> *immortal words of Snookie, herself: "I'm gonna do*
> *me. You do you."*

Acknowledging and accepting that there are other, equally valid viewpoints is a key to managing your behavior around others in a proactive, thoughtful, and modern way.

Day Twenty-Three Action

Having read Toni's account of her run-in with Jersey Shore's Village Yoga, what are your immediate judgments about this situation? Do you think you could suspend them? What questions might you ask yourself about your assumptions?

Think now about Diane from Village Yoga: What questions might you ask her that could help you see things from her perspective?

As you know, you can never change the minds of others; only they can do that. What you can do is open your own mind to their point of view, which might inspire them to reciprocate.

Manage Primitive Impulses Now
Shock and Awe

A great friend and colleague, and one of the world's most masterful coaches, Michael Bungay Stanier from boxofcrayons.biz, taught me to ask this simple question whenever I need to drill deeper into someone's description of a situation. It is the AWE question, which stands for "And What Else?"

I am continually amazed by how powerful this innocuous question is. Asking it allows people to vent, encourages them to dig down into the real issue, and motivates them to shift their perspective.

Just as important, it stops you from interjecting your own theories and viewpoints, without first fully understanding others. This enables you to see a new side to the issue—which is always helpful.

Ask it as often as you can: "And what else?"

Day 24

Open Your Heart
Be Available

> *One change always leaves the door open for the establishment of others.*
>
> —Niccolò Machiavelli

Today you'll tame:
- The unthinkingly ungenerous among us

Out of the blue, and impolitely, the boss was told the day before the global off-site that she was being moved to another territory—essentially, demoted—and that she should tell her team at the meeting.

Understandably, upon hearing this news, her mood was dangerously dark, and she knew it would be hard to hide. Still, she made a decision that, for the good of the others, she would not talk about her deepest feelings about her demotion with them—much as she wanted to bitch and moan and generally alert them to how screwed

(continued)

(continued)

up the company was for her, and in her view, for them too. Instead, she called her coach and offloaded on him.

She realized the only payoff for her from this was to be able to feel good that she had not "infected" her team with her bleak outlook, especially just before the trip. Besides, if she knew anything, it was that things, including how she felt, would change.

It was all too easy in writing this book to become very close-hearted about its content. I want everything in it to be *mine*, and so resist giving too much credit to the influence of others, those who have been major contributors to the wealth of wisdom and help I believe to be contained in it. It irks me somewhat to have to include the points of view on this subject of others, more clever or humorous. It is begrudgingly, then, that I offer you the words of John Cleese on the subject:

> *We all operate in two contrasting modes, which might be called open and closed. The open mode is more relaxed, more receptive, more exploratory, more democratic, more playful, and more humorous. The closed mode is the tighter, more rigid, more hierarchical, more tunnel-visioned. Most people unfortunately spend most of their time in the closed mode.*

Old Hats for Old Heads

No offense to Mr. Cleese, but this is not the first time I've heard this idea. It's a brilliantly simple one, one that I have also heard from friend and colleague Bruce Van Ryn–Bocking, who, as I told you earlier, is an expert in human behavior in the workplace. Bruce writes about the neuroscience of workplace relationships and workplace performance. Here's what he has to say:

> *Every person in love knows when their lover's heart is open and when it is closed. A closed heart usually precipitates the question, "What's wrong?" Not a good question to ask when the lover's heart is closed!!!*

When we speak about open and closed hearts, we are talking, once again, about the limbic system, that part of our brain that plays a pivotal role in mediating our emotions and relationships, and compels us to raise our young, live in families and villages, and work and play together.

All human beings (except some with a brain insufficiency in this regard) have the innate ability to know when another's heart is open or closed to them. This is because we are tribal in nature, and staying tuned to the mood of the alpha male or female in the tribe is essential to being allowed to stay in it, and therefore to our survival. This is not confined to lovers. It's also true of family members, friends, strangers, and people with whom we work.

I'm sure your own personal experience has shown you that not only is it more pleasurable to have a conversation with an open-hearted person, but that you are much more likely to do business with her, than with someone who is either indifferent or closed off to you.

The problem is that hearts open and close, depending on the weather, time of day, level of stress, anxiety about monthly sales targets, previous experiences, amount of sleep, and many other factors.

Therein lies the problem for us all: Whenever I meet up with colleagues, my heart may be at either end of the closed/open spectrum. And my coworker, client, customer, or boss will pick up on this intuitively, before I even open my mouth.

What to do about this?

My goal is to have an open heart whenever I engage with another person at work. I think it is the right (and clever) thing to do!

How to do this? Here are three tips that might work for you:

1. Ask friends and family if they think your heart is open or closed, and check their opinions against your self-perception. Also, notice when you are particularly self-critical or critical of others. Those are times when your heart is closed. Both of these exercise will help you to know when your heart is open or closed.

2. Develop the ability to open your heart intentionally. Most of us do this unconsciously, and can't say how. Set a conscious goal to open your heart, and then set about finding activities to help you do it. Here are a few ideas: listen to your favorite music, talk to a friend, go for a walk in nature, look at pictures of someone you love, write in a journal. Practice opening your heart. Practice with perfect strangers, like the teller at the bank or the clerk in the grocery store. These are low-risk situations that can help prepare you for the high-risk ones.

3. When all else fails, *pretend* your heart is open (fake it to make it). Put a twinkle in your eye when you look at people, and take note of the response you get, and what it does to your inner emotional state.

Says Bruce: "Opening your heart to others can mean that their reptilian brain puts you in their Friend category. That's the sweet place to work from."

Great advice from him, I think.

The Pain of Friendship

It turns out that people will suffer more pain on behalf of their close friends than they will for acquaintances, and sometimes for themselves.

Researchers believe that, in humans, social ties increase cooperation, so not only do friends and colleagues cooperate better than strangers, but they will also endure a high level of duress for each other. Indeed, some experiments suggest that we will endure more pain for our friends than for our family members. Perhaps the reason is that friends are a lot more important in earning us social benefits than are relatives, and so our primitive brain decides to make a bigger investment in friendships. Or it could be that we think we don't need to work as much on relationships with relatives, because family members have genes in common and so have a primitive predisposition to "stick together."

It's easy to imagine how this might play out in a family business. Where there are blood ties, there is a primitive predisposition to protect family members, but not necessarily to work on relationships with them. When it comes to coworkers we are friendly with, although we may have a primitive instinct to go the extra mile to build the social relationship, when push comes to shove, we will not protect them as we would our genetic family.

This dynamic can often cause people to feel they are treated grossly unfairly in family businesses and organizations, where during a crisis, even the most inept of the family is protected over even the most hard-working

(continued)

(*continued*)

and loyal "friends of the family," who can quickly find the company doors shut in their faces.

That said, a hierarchy exists even within the family, when it comes to the treatment that is dealt out. Sir Adrian Cadbury, former managing director and chairman of Cadbury–Schweppes, which started out as a family business in 1824, says:

> *At the heart of management of relationships in a family business lies the concept of fairness. Division and ruptures within the family can be caused only too easily through suspicion that some family members are benefiting at the expense of others, or that the contribution which some are making to the firm is not being properly recognized. The problem is to separate family judgments from business judgments.*

Keep Your Own Heart

Nature works in cycles and polarities; and we are all part of nature. Just as the seasons come and go, our hearts open and close. Having a bad day, being overtired or worried, or hanging around a grumpy person can all close our hearts. This can happen pretty easily. Remember that our primitive brain defaults to the negative when it is confused as to the action to take; otherwise, it will be indifferent (another fairly closed stance).

Opening our hearts can be more difficult—but worth the effort, especially in light of the fact that our moods are contagious. Keep in mind you could infect the entire workplace with your great, or bad, mood. If all of us take responsibility for our own moods, and we know how to keep our hearts open, even when dealing with grumpy people, we can help our community become a better place in which to live and work.

Day Twenty-Four Action

Is your heart open or closed, right now? Notice today when your heart feels open to people and situations, and when it feels closed to them. Where are you on that spectrum, and how would you like to change your position?

Here are more tips to help you shift to a more positive, open outlook:

♦ Spend time with someone optimistic.
♦ Read an article that has a positive outlook.
♦ Tell others about your hopes and aspirations.
♦ Avoid the evening news; it's usually only "bad" news.
♦ Google "kitten videos" and watch a few (seriously, it can melt the heart of the most closed individual).

Manage Primitive Impulses Now
Attack the Block

When people are behaving insufferably, !@#*ing us off big-time, our instinct is to either move away from that behavior (avoid it) or try to change it (fight it). Both of these responses come from us viewing the person as our enemy. Given that this is now our theory, it is likely that, no matter what behavior they display going forward, we will interpret it to fit with that diagnosis (again, best-fit thinking). Yes, you may be right; they could turn out to be against you. But by holding on to your initial judgment, and being unwilling to consider others, you shut the door to change. And it's dangerous to leave yourself unadaptable—just ask the dinosaurs. Oh, that's right, you can't; they're dead!

(continued)

(*continued*)

When you judge someone's behavior negatively, as being a threat to you, or simply because it annoys the living hell out of you try treating the person like a friend.

How do we do that, again?

Try one of those crinkly-eyed Duchenne smiles we talked about and practiced on Day Ten of the book. And here's a reminder of the killer move to add to your repertoire: *Have no agenda for their improvement.*

Now, I hear you protesting that when the actions of others can do you harm, you need to change them. But how successful have you been so far at changing other people's actions and points of view, anyway? Why not try dropping any agenda for changing the behaviors you don't like and instead commit to being curious about them. Ask people questions about what they are doing, rather than give an order. That way, at least, if they persist in doing what seems threatening to you, you will have a lot more information about it, so that you know how to act on it more effectively—and that's powerful.

Day 25

Give

Receive

We make a living by what we get. We make a life by what we give.

—Winston Churchill

Today you'll tame:

♦ Age-old advice

There are some people at your workplace who, when asked a question, will deliver a 10-minute mini-lecture as an answer.

Often, we find that they never really understood our motivation for asking the question in the first place, and misheard it in any case. And though their answer may have been entertaining and interesting, it was, essentially, useless. We find this kind of "help" from them just plain !@#$ing annoying!

(continued)

> (*continued*)
>
> Then there are the people at your workplace who, when asked a question, say, "That's a good question. What do you think about it?"
>
> Then they listen, accept your thoughts, sometimes ask more questions, and finally offer their ideas to help you adjust your thinking.
>
> Which approach do you like best?

You may well be aware that many of the oldest and wisest religious, philosophical, moral, and ethical models suggest that giving is better than receiving. And if you define living a long and healthy life as a great thing, then this principle is on the money—to an extent.

Better to Give . . .

Giving increases the giver's longevity.

The are two kinds of giving I am talking about here. First is *instrumental support*; for example, when you lend a hand, pitch in, offer to pick up the slack, and generally do whatever it takes to help move *others* toward their goals. Then there's *emotional support*, which revolves around making other people feel wanted, cared for, and listened to. Often, this takes the form of being emotionally empathetic—you join them in the emotional place. Or equally useful, you are cognitively empathetic; you accept the emotional state they are in, but you don't go there with them.

Whether you're offering instrumental or emotional support, one thing remains the same: *You can't engage in either of them on your own.* You have to make contact with the person you are helping, and at times create a connection with him. This is social.

Health scientists have known for some time now that social contact can have a measurable impact on protecting people's health. It boosts the immune system, lowers the frequency of colds and other infections, and speeds wound healing. In short, it promotes longevity for the *giver* in a significant way.

. . . Than to Receive

It turns out, however, that not all social contact is created equal. Ironically, the health benefits of social contact may be gained only by those on the giving end. Receiving support, while helpful in some ways, isn't always a total blessing.

Intuitively, we believe that helping others makes them feel better, because we are connected and that connection raises the levels of important neurotransmitters—dopamine and oxytocin among others—in *our* brains, giving us a compelling and warm sensation overall.

The recipients on the other end of the interaction, however, may come to feel dependent, and of low status; they may also experience guilt or anxiety, and feel they are a burden, all of which can adversely affect their brain, by lowering the levels of neurotransmitters. If such a state is sustained over long enough periods of time, it can lead to depression (both emotionally and physically within the immune system).

So while giving help to others has many healthful benefits to *givers*—reduces stress, improves both mental and physical health, stimulates a sense of belonging and well-being, increases happiness/decreases depression, promotes cardiovascular health, and boosts the immune system—*receiving* help provides no such benefits!

This is not to say that you should not help your colleagues, in order to "save" them from mental, emotional, and physical collapse; and, generally speaking, leave them in the %^&*. It is to say we can nuance how we offer help, to mitigate any loss of self-worth that the recipient of that help may experience.

Take My Advice; I'm Not Using It!

A lot of our daily conversations involve giving and taking advice. You talk with a friend about a new movie he has already seen and he recommends that you go see it, too. Two other friends want to go to that new Latino-Inuit crossover restaurant in the neighborhood, and you tell them to avoid it "like the plague," because you tried the ceviche-seal burrito and it gave you food poisoning.

Giving advice to people we work with is one of the main ways we attempt to help others. How useful is our advice? Let's take a look.

There are, perhaps, four types of advice:

1. **Recommendation to move toward an option:** "Do it this way."
2. **Recommendation to avoid an option:** "*Don't* do it that way!"
3. **Information we previously didn't have that could affect a choice:** "I tried that workaround earlier today, before you got here, and messed up the software further."
4. **Suggestions on how to make a choice:** "Draw a quadrant matrix and place high- to low-value outcome on one axis, and resource drain on the other. Then plot each potential strategy within the matrix, and do an analysis based on where they fall."

In general, all these types of advice can be useful, to some degree. However, the advice that is least offensive and most useful to a majority of us is number 3—getting information that presents data, and thus, options, we might otherwise not have known about.

Instinctive about Choices

There are a few primitive reasons why getting information is more valuable to people than other kinds of advice. For one thing, when someone makes a recommendation for or against a particular option, a decision maker may feel as if he has to relinquish a bit of his independence in making a choice. Lack of choice or autonomy lowers the level of dopamine in the brain and causes the advisee to initiate a retreat response from the advisor. The advisor is now seen as an enemy, even though he was only offering his best advice. This leads us back to the negative consequences sometimes experienced by those receiving help.

Recommendations about how to make a choice may also cause the decision maker to feel a loss of independence; and furthermore, can lower his estimation of his rank or status, as compared to that of the advisor. In this scenario, too, the dopamine level decreases, the retreat response kicks in, and the helper is regarded as lowering the status of the one he was trying, in fact, to help (and who may already be feeling pretty low about the whole situation). Remember, the primitive brain gets very upset and frustrated, and often aggressive, when things do not go as it would like.

But when advice comes in the form of information, the decision maker can maintain his autonomy; he is not being told what to do. He retains his status in his own eyes, and potentially raises it because he can decide to take or leave the advice, implying that he is competent to make his own decisions.

Information is, simply, knowledge we did not have before, and so it can make us aware of particular dimensions of making a decision we had not yet considered. It is, therefore, of interest to the neocortex; it stimulates it into activity, thus countermanding the activity in which the brain stem may be involved—often, the impulse (and related feelings) to destroy the problem and everything linked to it.

Being given information makes people feel more confident in the decision they ultimately make. The information provides what they need to know to develop reasons for or against a particular option. There is a lot of evidence to suggest that people feel better about the decisions they make when they are able to give a reason for their choice. In addition, making that choice sends the brain a hit of dopamine; thus, getting information provides a feel-good factor and a justification for a choice.

Day Twenty-Five Action

Think about the last time you gave advice. What type of advice was it? Now think about what additional information you could have given that would have aided the recipient of your advice in making his own decision.

Make a commitment to yourself to watch for the next opportunity to give advice, and make a point of giving *only* information—nothing else, even if pushed. How does that feel and how does it help?

Manage Primitive Impulses Now
Here's My Two Cents

Take it from me: Stop giving advice. People don't like it when you do. It makes some of them, literally, red in the face. Others will just avoid you, tune out, or switch off, when you start to give it. You should know that by now. Besides, most people don't follow the advice they're given, anyway. And, if they did, and it didn't work out, they have you to blame.

On the other hand, offering information, when accurate, is always useful.

Some people find that simply giving their full attention, listening intently, and asking a few simple questions can help people through a lot of tricky situations.

Might this work for you?

Day 26

Manage Your Disappointment
Dealing with the Letdown

I'd be lying if I said I wasn't angry some days.

—Monica Lewinsky

Today you'll tame:

- Your original motivations versus the newer outcomes

Three years into the job and Kristin was still not getting what she had expected out of it.

Every six months or so she would ask management if she could move the work she was doing closer to what she had believed it would be when she had taken the post. And every six months management would assure her that she would be allowed to work on the projects of interest for her, eventually. Yet year after year, it never happened.

Kristin had lived with hope for four years, but this fifth one had hit her badly.

She was now taking weeks off from work, feeling low and lethargic; and when she was at work, she was irritable. At times, she had even been irrationally aggressive with coworkers—so much so that she had been given a written warning about it.

Finally, after talking to a counselor, she managed to put her finger on the problem: Disappointment!

Her next move was to decide whether she was going to live with the disappointment in her job or move on to another.

In everything we do, there is what we expect and what we actually get. When reality delivers less than you expected you can feel disappointment. When reality delivers more than you expected you can feel delight. There are those who say, "I don't have expectations; that way I can never be disappointed." Others suggest that we live like the birds, the trees, and the water in the steams, without expectation—that we just "be." I like that idea—as an ideal—but it's difficult to practice, as it's just not the way our brains are built.

It is expectation that gets us up in the morning, and expectation that leads us to open the door of the refrigerator, turn the key to start the car, and open that e-mail from our best customer.

You wouldn't be reading this book if you didn't expect that there would be something of value in it. You can no more live without expectations than you can live without air to breathe. Even Buddhists, who spend years in meditation to learn to let go of expectations, do so in the expectation that they will achieve this goal.

Goals

Without expectation, we have no objectives, can set no goals, and draw no road map to lead us to the days, weeks and years ahead.

The real challenge is managing the goals we set, the expectations that others have of us and that we have of ourselves, the targets we shoot for, and our feelings around all of these.

Human behavior is powerfully influenced by the sometimes uneasy balance between our primitive brain's reward and punishment systems. In general, most of us pursue activities that are pleasurable or rewarding, while we avoid those that are punishing or threatening. We do this by selecting appropriate goals, initiating the behaviors required to achieve those goals, and then recognizing the signals that the goals have been achieved. If achieving a goal provides a stable and beneficial environment, then that achievement reinforces the behavior leading to it (the end justifies the means). Conversely, if achieving a goal proves toxic, then in the future we suppress and avoid the behavior leading up to it.

This system appears to be initiated by central reward and punishment pathways in the brain. These pathways are closely integrated with systems for learning, remembering, and motivating. They form the basis for reptilian brain drives such as hunger, thirst, and sex, but also contribute to more complex emotional/cognitive states, such as hope and disappointment.

Clearly, in humans at least, reward and punishment systems can involve conscious thought and behavior. For example, we may consciously defer anticipated rewards: "I'll have my chocolate cookie during my coffee break as a reward for making it through to 11:00 AM" (a relatively minor suppressive activity carried out with the prospect of a future pleasurable goal). Conversely, we may seize upon a momentary pleasure despite knowledge of future punishment for taking our reward now: "This job sucks! I'm having my cookie now! In fact, I'll have five, 'cause my work is so boring."

Reward and punishment systems generate moods and emotions that can overpower rational thought. Rewarding events can result in a range of pleasurable feelings (joy, contentment, hope, elation), whereas punishing events generate unpleasant feelings (hunger, fear, guilt, despair). And when we expect reward and don't get it, we are disappointed; conversely, when we expect punishment and don't get it, we are relieved.

People Can Disappoint

I once heard Ricky Gervais, comedian and creator of the NBC series *The Office*, talk about how he sees David Brent, the central character of the original BBC UK version of the series. He said something along the lines of: "Your blind spot is often the distance between how you see yourself and how the rest of the world sees you. If there is a chasm between the two, you may have a problem."

When we are unaware of the gap that exists between what is expected of our performance and what we actually deliver, the opportunity for disappointment is huge.

Too often, our solution is to say, about others: "They need to be more realistic, or less demanding." And about ourselves we think, "I'm a genius; they just don't appreciate me!" Neither of these is a very intelligent solution to a primitive brain problem.

Expect Disappointment

Disappointment at work comes when expectations are not met, either our own or someone else's. The problem is not that people let us down, or that we don't accomplish all that we ought to have done; the problem is that we keep wishing for what we think *should be*, instead of managing *what is*.

As long as we keep expecting something other than reality, we'll end up unprepared for what we actually get, or what actually happens.

It is true that we could not function very well without expectations. We expect that people will stop at red lights and go when they turn green. We expect that employees will come to the office on workdays. There is nothing wrong with such expectations.

At work, our expectations of ourselves and others help us to move more easily through our days, each adding to the performance of our colleagues and not getting in each other's way or stepping on each other's toes.

But what if one of the things that I expect to happen doesn't? It should. But it doesn't. I am stopped at a traffic light; then the light turns green. I know that means that on the intersecting road, the light has turned red. I expect drivers on that side to stop. Nevertheless, I look before I proceed, because I know that sometimes people run red lights.

The point is, it is better for me (and them, for that matter) if I accept that sometimes people don't do what I think they are supposed to do, whether it is because they won't or can't or didn't know they were supposed to.

And if I expect that I will be disappointed at times, that the universe won't always take my expectations into account, then my ability to anticipate problems will improve. I won't be shocked when things don't turn out as I expected; and even better, I will be disappointed less often.

Day Twenty-Six Action

Today, be on the alert for disappointment, both yours and that of others. You'll find a lot of it, because we all have a lot of expectations. When you notice that expectations have not been met, start by saying, "That must be disappointing," or "That's a disappointment," to describe how you or others must be feeling. It is amazing how powerful it is when you can name a feeling accurately. And note that naming it is not being negative; it is just being accurate. Recognizing and naming disappointment allows the primitive brain to give up control to the neocortex, so that you can get on with problem solving.

Suggest to your colleagues that naming disappointment, as well as other negative and positive feelings (when they show up) become a routine part of your company culture. This does not mean "naming and shaming," or celebrating every pleasurable experience; but rather acknowledging that you and others had expected one thing and gotten another. Maybe you are delighted by the results. Maybe you are feeling a little let down. Either way, try following the five steps below to help guide the conversation.

Manage Primitive Impulses Now
Five Steps to Relieve Disappointment

When you have experienced behavior that disappoints, and you'd like to avoid it in the future:

1. Describe your expectations of behavior.
2. Describe the behavior you experienced.
3. Explain how you feel about the difference between the two.
4. Ask for feedback.
5. Listen.

Often, by following these steps, you will learn new information that helps you see a different side to the behavior. People may intimate that they will change their

(*continued*)

(*continued*)

behavior to better suit you—without you having to ask, demand, or beg. You may even get an apology. Once in a while you may be told by someone that she doesn't care about your feelings. That can be difficult to hear. But once you know she feels this way, you can decide what you are going to do about it.

Day 27

Values Trump Rules

Society's Expectations

Culture eats strategy for breakfast.

—Peter Drucker

Today you'll tame:

♦ Bureaucratic rules for our primeval behaviors

The company had clear values, and one of them was around "wise spending." Everyone had a shared understanding of what this meant.

So when it came to the financial crunch and the group had to rein in expenses by 10 percent, no one had to put a committee together and take up valuable time and resources hatching an elaborate strategy to make personal cuts to spending.

The CEO simply reminded his team at the yearly meeting about their shared wise-spending value and thanked them for finding their own ways to "live it," especially when on company business.

(continued)

(*continued*)

He gave a few examples of what he would be doing: When having dinner with a client, he would buy a bottle that was a few dollars cheaper than he would normally spend. When traveling to group meetings, he would check schedules ahead of time to, if he could, share a taxi to the hotel with anyone else on the team—or simply take the shuttle.

He ended by saying, "But it's up to you how *you* do this."

Expenses dropped 15 percent.

Rules are created by tribal leaders (parents, teachers, employers, elected officials) to control the self-centered behaviors of the reptilian brain. "Don't steal" is designed to control the urge to take food from others; "don't hit," to alter the fight response from using fists to using words. All such rules are in support of sustaining the tribe.

But rules only work when they are respected, or when the parental figure is around to enforce them. Otherwise, as every child and parent knows, when the adult is out of sight, and can't see what the child is doing, breaking the rules can be fun, or at least give an added adrenaline rush to an activity (important to adrenaline junkies who self-medicate).

Every few weeks, there is an article in the business press about a company leader who broke the rules. Remember Enron and WorldCom? Yes, the execs at these companies got caught, and some even got punished; and in the meantime, billions of dollars were lost, never to be recovered.

So, while rules serve an important purpose, in that most people follow them (most of us are good tribal citizens), they don't work all the time.

Rules are great for telling people what to do and how to behave under a specific set of circumstances. But it is *values* that give us direction on an ongoing basis, regardless of circumstances.

Rules and Artificial Intelligence

Why can honoring values be a better way of living and working? Remember that our primitive brain needs to make many, many decisions in short periods of time, and under circumstances that have not yet been described or experienced, and that can change rapidly. Under such conditions, rules may not be the most useful. Looking for, and finding, the right rule to fit every circumstance may be too slow a process. That is why many rules are made after the fact, after the tribe understands what has gone wrong, and why, and tries to prevent it from happening again.

Recall the company at the beginning of the chapter that had to cut expenses by 10 percent. Imagine the many, many rules that would need to be in place to cover each and every expense of each and every employee. Now imagine trying to police those rules. That task alone would require a team of on-site auditors, and drive up expenses. Next, imagine the timeline, and when contravention of the rules might be exposed—could be days, weeks, or months after the fiscal quarter has ended. Now imagine what the company might do with transgressors: Fine them? Shame them? Fire them? Finally, imagine the effect on morale, and productivity, if the company has to replace key people.

As it happens, our primitive intelligence does not work via a multitude of rules, either. Understandably therefore, Artificial Intelligence (meaning the study and design of making intelligent machines and systems that can perceive their environment and take actions that maximize their chances of success, their ability to reach a set goal) is being consistently improved as it is designed to increasingly mirror our own: Rather than programming thousands of rules, programmers design simple machines with just three or four rules. Then they give the machines a goal and a memory, so that they can learn. Here is the design again:

- ◆ A few rules
- ◆ A goal
- ◆ Memory

Engineers have discovered that when these machines are put into complex and even dynamically evolving environments, they are able to learn, adapt, and progress to a goal much more efficiently than multiple-rule-oriented artificial intelligence technologies. These machines can improvise, and even surprise the people who invented them, by evolving in unpredictable ways.

Office Talk

Sometimes it is easier for us to invoke rules rather than engage in a more complex discussion of what our values are (both individual and shared), and how those values affect our behaviors in the workplace.

I heard a story about a hospital janitor who decided, against the rules, not to clean a corridor floor one day. Why? Because, he said, "A patient was up and about that day for the first time," and the janitor decided it was better for this person to be able to walk without danger of slipping on a wet floor than to have a spotless floor. As you might imagine, he had some explaining to do to his supervisors, and he risked punishment. But his personal value was "help people to become well."

Another of his values came into play one day when he failed to vacuum the visitor's area carpet. Why?

Because he learned that a family had just been given some devastating news and were consoling each other in the space, and he valued their need for privacy and quiet while they grappled with that news, over the rule to clean the carpet.

And, in contrast, in a lesson from history: Adolf Eichmann, the Nazi SS lieutenant colonel given the task of facilitating and managing the mass deportation of Jews, Romani, Communists, Poles, homosexuals, people with disabilities, and a multitude of political and religious opponents to extermination camps during the Second World War, was asked at his Jerusalem trial (conducted under the auspices of Israel's Nazi and Nazi Collaborators [Punishment] Law) if it had been difficult to send millions to their deaths. He replied, that it was easy. His language made it easy. Eichmann and his fellow officers coined their own name for their language. They called it *amtssprache*—office talk. With this language they could deny responsibility for their actions. So if anybody asked, why did you do it? They could say, I had to; superiors' orders; policy. It's the law.

Eichmann gave what was known as the "Nuremberg plea," claiming he was "just following superiors' orders" (i.e., the rules). (Let's not overlook here that Eichmann's personal values were fully aligned with those of Hitler's, and he was a proponent of the most vehement Nazi viewpoint.)

Your work, I realize, has nothing to do with Eichmann or the extremes of that situation; however, Nazism does provide a very clear (if disturbing) example of how, by creating a culture that values following the rules, you

(*continued*)

> (*continued*)
>
> risk also creating a culture that loses its moral compass or code. We should all avoid the temptation, in whatever work we do, to fall back on the Eichmann defense—"It's my job"; "They told me to do it"; "I'm only following company policy"; "I have to finish my shift at 5:30 so talk to the next guy"—as a means of shielding ourselves from doing what is best and right. Sometimes it means breaking a rule in the book to honor one of our own personal values, written in blood.

Organizational Intelligence

The organizations where we work can often create long lists of tasks they want their employees to do (think: employee handbooks, manuals, training binders, notices, etc.). What rules tend *not* to do is help people discuss and embrace a handful of values (the most important "rules").

Highly effective teams, and indeed companies, are given a goal, a few rules (budget, timeline, equipment, etc.) that set boundaries and a means to record and share their work, and then are given the freedom to explore and be creative. Importantly, they also have a set of shared values. Zappos is an excellent example of a company that embraces a set of core values. Founder and CEO Tony Hsieh, says "If we get the culture right, then everything else, including the customer service, will fall into place." The proof is on the bottom line: Zappos hit the billion-dollar mark in sales two years ahead of schedule; it also debuted on *Fortune* magazine's list of Top 100 Companies to Work For.

Companies that stress the importance of embracing values will benefit when decisions have to be made for which there are no rules to fall back on; at those times, each member of the team can rely on those shared values, and use them as a guide to make appropriate decisions.

Remember I told you about the year I spent as president of my business networking group, and that, when asked by other members what they should do, I simply reminded them of our core, shared value: "Do what maximizes giving to others"?

If you put together a group of people who share values, and then give them a goal, they will often use ingenuity that they, and you, didn't even know they had.

On the flip side, if you're not getting the output you want from individuals or teams, there are potentially four reasons.

1. The team doesn't know what the goals are.
2. The team members don't share the same values.
3. The team doesn't have the resources it needs.
4. The team isn't learning from its mistakes and successes.

How about your work environment? Do people (including you) struggle with one of the four problems above?

And how about the cultures you lead—friends or family or teams or clubs? Do you lead by creating rules or modeling values?

Rules for Collapse

Research In Motion (RIM), maker of the iconic BlackBerry, created a device that sent encrypted e-mail to and from its customers' devices. By August 2007, RIM stock had risen to $228 before splitting 3:1. The company valued security and secrecy, as did its business, government, and military customers. But by August 2012, RIM's stock was languishing below $7, and its market share for smartphones had fallen precipitously against that of the iPhone and Android.

(continued)

(continued)

Two things had changed for RIM: Smartphones had been discovered by consumers, and competitors had entered the market. What did Apple and Google know about the values of the average consumer that RIM didn't discover, until too late?

The average smartphone consumer (primarily teens and young adults) valued convenience (both for connecting with friends and browsing) and status (earned by having the latest and most fascinating apps). They didn't, so much, value security. It took RIM a long time to open up their approval process and their software so that developers could easily write apps for BlackBerry devices. In February 2012, RIM announced that it had over 60,000 apps in its app store; at about the same time, Apple announced that it had available over 550,000 apps.

Company values all start with the customer. There needs to be alignment with the customers' values at every level of the organization, from the lowest-paid employee to the CEO and on to suppliers and strategic partners.

Take a Break

Consider the staff break room. How many of us have experienced a scenario similar to this? A manager puts up a sign that reads, "Please Clean the Microwave after You Use It." Then another: "Do Not Put Your Feet on the Tables." Then a third: "Don't Eat Other People's Food." All these rules, and the myriad more little lunchroom do's and don'ts that your manager madly writes, prints out, and posts, attempt to codify a single value: Have respect for the place where people eat, and for all who share that place.

Rather than declare a common value, such as, "Thanks for Respecting Our Common Spaces," and discussing what that may mean, most rule makers spend their time trying to control the reptilian brain, while each person's reptilian brain is intently looking for ways to escape that control. We are all brilliant rule breakers when we need to be—always able to reverse-engineer a great reason as to why the rule is not applicable or valid for us in this specific situation. We can even invent technologies that will help us circumvent the rules. Those radar detectors that busy execs have in their BMWs help them get from meeting to meeting without getting a ticket for breaking the speed limit.

Better for each of us to monitor and regulate our own reptilian brain. After all, I know best what mischief my primitive brain wants to get up to, and how it will try to make me do that. It is only my values that I can rely on to help me manage it. If I share those values with others around me, then we'll all get along just fine.

Day Twenty-Seven Action

Which are the rules at your office that you just can't abide? Do you know why you want to break them? Or why you may well be flouting your rebellion to them openly on a regular basis?

Take a look again at your list of tribes that you made on Day Fifteen, and examined on Day Eighteen. Examine the values that these tribes hold as most important. Now think about your personal core values—what you believe to be most important in life. Do any of your personal values conflict with your work tribe's values?

Are there some rules at work that you can now see uphold the values of a tribe but conflict with your personal values? If so, what are you thinking of doing to resolve the conflict? Will you continue to be annoyed by the rules, break the rules, or do something else, perhaps?

Manage Primitive Impulses Now
Find Their Solution

Do you feel you need to impose rules on people? Instead:

1. Pose the problem.
2. Ask them to come up with a solution that makes sense to them.
3. Listen to it and share any further ideas you have.
4. Check that the final solution reflects both your values.

Day 28

Expand Your Tribe

Global Village

One good reason to only maintain a small circle of friends is that three out of four murders are committed by people who know the victim.

—George Carlin

Today you'll tame:
♦ Your old-world village mentality

Bruce's friend Stephen had just retired from 30 years of teaching. They were in their favorite coffee shop, talking about retirement and life after work, when Stephen mentioned that he was thinking about teaching English in Asia for a couple of years. He had always wanted to travel, and this seemed like a great way to facilitate that.

Bruce mentioned that his daughter, Lauren, was teaching English as a Second Language (ESL) in South Korea, and happened to be home for a visit. Perhaps Stephen would like to chat with her about her experiences there?

(continued)

(*continued*)

Stephen liked that idea, so Bruce asked Lauren to come over for lunch on a day Stephen could come as well. The lunch date arrived. Stephen showed up first. As the two men were chatting, Lauren came into the room.

Bruce was amazed to see Lauren greet Stephen as she would a long-lost friend—huge smile on her face, energy in her voice, and warm and welcoming body language.

Bruce recognized that Lauren clearly shared some values with Stephen around education and travel—they were "kindred spirits." All the same, he thought, "I never do that, unless the person is a favorite relative or very close and well-loved friend." Which got him to thinking further: "Perhaps Lauren's tribe is a lot larger than mine. Perhaps it includes the entire human race!"

Why do we hang out in groups? Is it because we love to give to others, or because we love to gain from others? Some people say there's no such thing as a selfless act; that any time we do something to help another person, we get something in return, even if it's just a warm fuzzy feeling. And as you've read in previous chapters, neurochemically speaking, that is true. Well, it may be true in other more tangible ways, too.

Social Advantage

In 2009 the BBC reported their findings on a study of 10,000 U.S. students over a period of 35 years that concluded the more friends you have, the more you earn. The wealthiest people were those who had the most friends at school. Each extra school friend was the equivalent of adding 2 percent to the salary. The research said this was due to the fact that the workplace is a social setting, and that those with the best social skills prosper in management and teamwork.

If having a wide circle of friends is taken as a popularity indicator, does that mean the more friends you have, the more successful and happy you will be? Or is it possible to have too many? How many friends on Facebook do you *really* have?

One study by Facebook found that the average Facebook user has around 229 friends, broken down as follows: around 22 percent of the total friends list is made up of old high school friends; 12 percent is extended family; 10 percent, coworkers; 9 percent, college friends; 8 percent, immediate family; 7 percent, people from extracurricular groups; and 2 percent, neighbors.

The study also found that the typical Facebook user has never actually met about 7 percent of their Facebook "friends" in real life; and on average, users have met 3 percent of their "friends" just once.

Is there an optimum number of "real" friends?

Closer Than "on Average"

The average number of significant social relationships is about 150, says leading anthropologist Robin Dunbar: "It's the number of people that you know as persons, and you know how they fit into your social world, and they know how you fit into theirs. They are a group of people to which you have an obligation of friendship."

"They," Robin says, usually consist of an inner circle of five "core" people and an additional layer of 10. That makes 15 people—some of which will probably be family members— who are your central group. Outside that group, in the next circle, are another 35, and then another 100 on the outside of that circle. That's just one person's social world.

Friendships help us develop as people, says Mark Vernon, author of *The Philosophy of Friendship*, but the term *friend* covers a whole range of relationships. You have a very close friendship with your partner; but with others your friendship may be due to a common interest or history, or simply having children the same age.

There's a limit to how many close friends you can have, and it's probably between 6 and 12, Mark says.

We all understand the benefit we gain by living and working with the right-for-us group of people. And we can all understand that if we can make that group bigger, we will have more power at our disposal.

The World Is Your Oyster

It used to be, not too long ago, that the only opportunities for friendship, mating, and working all occurred within a few miles of where you lived. That's because it took too long to travel to the neighboring village to make the trip worth our while. So our village was our world. And chances are that the people who lived in that village were very much like us—same religion and similar values, beliefs, and customs. That made us all predictable, and that predictability made us all safe.

In addition, many people's friends were much like them—same skin color, same language, similar interests, and so on.

In our modern world, with global-reach communication technologies and travel capabilities, we can, and often do, scale our villages exponentially. We can have a global village of friends, coworkers, clients, and customers across the world, 24/7. It is an industrial model (more productivity for less expense) of the village. For some, this is a very powerful way to work and live. At the same time, if you're working in a highly diverse group, you're fighting your primitive tribal nature to stick with "your own kind." My hunch is that, in the global village of the future, the most successful people will be those who can do just that.

Taking Orders

I believe Apple talks about "two-pizza teams"—that is, keeping teams small enough so that they can be fed with just two pizzas.

It's an economical idea, on many levels.

Remember that our evolutionary psychology wants to get us the best advantage for the least expense. And when you've got a small group of people from the same backgrounds and culture, you share a kind of shorthand; you already understand many of the same things; and you don't need to constantly formalize things—that's less thinking needed right there, and so fewer calories to find and consume. With fewer people you stand a better chance of getting together face-to-face. And with like-minded people, when you communicate, you understand each other very well. In all ways, your relationships are more predictable. If you have a question about something, you ask, and are confident you will understand the answer. Way less confusing.

Small Is Beautiful

There are centuries of evidence to support the idea that small groups are the most efficient. We humans have worked in small groups, usually anything from 5 to 15 people, as hunters and gatherers and farmers, for hundreds of generations—think army squads, juries, committees, sports teams, and many more.

Such groups are small enough so that the contribution of each member makes a noticeable difference. It is fairly easy to monitor a group when everyone in it understands or is on board with the common objective and the criteria for success.

Maybe human nature would say that if you want a team bigger than 15, you should create a subteam. Start a satellite group and see if you can lose the busywork and bureaucracy that inevitably accompany oversized teams. And if we want to extend our reach and power, we need to be part of or have influence on a number of different teams, rather than have to manage a single, very large one.

Day Twenty-Eight Action

Notice who is part of your inner circle at work. Are they all from roughly the same background as you?

Who do you know at work that is different from you and your closest professional friends, that you can invite to join your team, attend the meeting, or just hang out with more often, in order to bring a more diverse perspective to your company "village." These may be individuals you've been indifferent to, or have even been avoiding, or you see as way above or below you in the organizational hierarchy.

Manage Primitive Impulses Now
Get a More Global View

It you've made it this far in the book, it could be that you are starting to think a little too much like me. In fact, maybe you picked up this book in the first place because you and I are similar in many ways. Maybe we are from the same tribe? Maybe through this book we've become part of the same tribe. Either way, I recommend that you go forth and invite different points of view on everything we've been talking about and doing together.

There are a lot of other people out there you could ask for help in taming your primitive brain and managing some of the most impulsive behaviors at work. Now is as good a time as any to chat with others about everything you've discovered about yourself and others by reading this book; get their viewpoint on it. Maybe find someone at work you don't usually talk to about this kind of topic and start a conversation with her. Ask someone outside of your workplace how people behave where he works. Or log on to the Internet and connect with people who work on the other side of the globe; and ask what impulsive behaviors they see in their neck of the woods, and how they manage them.

They may all think that what you've been learning and experiencing is a crock. Or they may be really interested in it and want to borrow the book from you, to find out more themselves. Finally, they may have some interesting insights that will help you to further develop your skill in managing your impulsive behaviors and those of the people you work with.

Conclusion
The Way Forward

It is easier to prevent bad habits than to change them.
—Benjamin Franklin

If you've followed all or even just a few of the actions, tips, and techniques laid out in this book then I will lay down good money that you are seeing people's behavior (including your own) in a very different light. You might even be having very different reactions to them: cooler, calmer, more assertive, and less impulsive. And people have very probably commented on how refreshing this is.

Your question now may be: "How do I keep this up? What's the plan, Stan?"

Maybe you've already noticed that your primitive brain has no interest in planning for the future; its only concern is with dealing with today, based on how yesterday turned out.

Our limbic system, which has a memory of all the *most impactful yesterdays,* rewards us when we behave accordingly to those. Our reptilian brain, in contrast, has an inherited structure based on *many millennia of yesterdays,* and when triggered, rewards us for adhering to this ancient code.

In short, our behavior is triggered based on our past and on our genetics; a pattern of action plays out, and we are rewarded at the end of it, which serves to enforce the pattern.

How do we create new habits of behavior that will give us better results than our instinctive behaviors, given that these instinctive responses are enacted in our primitive brain and cannot be planned?

Here's the answer:

We can't!

Understand now that the environments that trigger your primitive behaviors will *always* trigger those behaviors. And when that behavior gets a familiar result, your primitive brain will feel rewarded, and thus the behavior will be reinforced, thereby heating up the desire for more and similar triggers.

What you *can* do is decide which of your behaviors you most want to adjust. Ask yourself, "What triggers those behaviors?" Then ask, "Where, when, and by whom are those behaviors most likely to be triggered?"

♦ One way to temper a habit is to seek other environments that don't support the triggers you are trying to change.

     For some, however, avoiding these environments would be tantamount to avoiding life, so take a look at the next idea.

♦ A second way is to make the commitment that when you are in those environments, and are triggered, to mindfully choose another, less instinctual behavior, and then to reward yourself for making that wiser choice.

     For those of you for whom the trigger is so strong that the behavior plays out before you can choose another, take a look at the next idea.

♦ A third option is to let people know what triggers set you off and what they can expect from you when this happens. Maybe they will make an effort to change the environment a little for you, to help you out. Or forewarned, they can avoid you.

Your instincts (and everyone else's) won't ever change. Some are good, some are bad, but all are hardwired in your brain. Although you can't change them, you can learn to manage these impulses better. You need to keep your eye on yourself, recognize what causes you to react in ways you'd rather not, and then change your environment and/or your responses to it. If you are at all like me, this will take practice.

The good news is, you have the rest of your life for that.

Further Reading and Resources

A list of books and articles referred to, consulted, or of related interest.

Anton Wilson, Robert. *Quantum Psychology: How Brain Software Programs You & Your World*. Las Vegas, NV: New Falcon Publications, 1990.

Ibid. *Prometheus Rising*. Las Vegas, NV: New Falcon Publications, 2009.

Ardrey, Robert, and Ardrey, Berdine. *The Territorial Imperative: A Personal Inquiry into the Animal Origins of Property and Nations*. New York, NY: Atheneum, 1966.

Arendt, Hannah. *Eichmann in Jerusalem: A Report on the Banality of Evil*. New York, NY: Penguin Classics, 2006.

Bandler, Richard, and Grinder, John. *The Structure of Magic* (2 vols). Palo Alto, CA: Science and Behavior Books, 1976.

Barash, David P. *Homo Mysterious: Evolutionary Puzzles of Human Nature*. Oxford, UK: Oxford University Press, 2012.

Barrett, Louise. *Beyond the Brain—How Body and Environment Shape Animal and Human Minds*. Princeton, NJ: Princeton University Press, 2011.

Beckhard, Richard. *Organization Development: Strategies and Models*. Boston, MA: Addison-Wesley, 1969.

Bickerton, Derek. *Adam's Tongue—How Humans Made Language, and Language Made Humans*. New York, NY: Hill and Wang, 2010.

Bowden, Mark. *Winning Body Language: Control the Conversation, Command Attention, and Convey the Right Message—without Saying a Word*. New York, NY: McGraw-Hill, 2010.

Ibid. *Winning Body Language for Sales Professionals: Control the Conversation and Connect with Your Customer—without Saying a Word*. New York, NY: McGraw-Hill, 2012.

Cannon, Walter. *Bodily Changes in Pain, Hunger, Fear, and Rage: An Account of Recent Researches into the Function of Emotional Excitement*. New York, NY: D. Appleton and Co., 1915.

Carter, Rita. *Mapping the Mind*. Berkeley, CA: University of California Press, 2000.

Dalai Lama, and Ekman, Paul. *Emotional Awareness: Overcoming the Obstacles to Psychological Balance and Compassion.* New York, NY: Times Books, 2008.

Damasio, Antonio. *Descartes' Error: Emotion, Reason, and the Human Brain.* London, UK: Penguin, 2005.

Darwin, Charles. *Works of Charles Darwin: Including On the Origin of Species, The Descent of Man, The Expression of Emotions in Man and Animals.* Boston, MA: Mobile Reference (Kindle edition), 2000.

Dawkins, Richard. *The Selfish Gene.* Oxford, UK: Oxford University Press, 1989.

De Becker, Gavin. *The Gift of Fear and Other Survival Signals That Protect Us from Violence.* New York, NY: Dell, 1999.

Dilts, Robert. *Sleight of Mouth.* Capitola, CA: Meta Publications, 1999.

Duchenne, Guillaume-Benjamin. *Mécanisme de la Physionomie Humaine: Où, Analyse Électro-Physiologique de L'expression des Passions.* Charlston, SC: Nabu Press, 2010.

Ekman, Paul. *Emotions Revealed: Recognizing Faces and Feelings to Improve Communication and Emotional Life.* New York, NY: Holt, 2007.

Gleick, James. *Chaos: Making a New Science.* London, UK: Penguin Books, 2008.

Hackman, J. R. "What Makes for a Great Team?" APA Science Briefs, http://www.apa.org/science/about/psa/2004/06/hackman.aspx, accessed November 5, 2012.

Harrison, Freya, Sciberras, James, and James, Richard. "Strength of Social Tie Predicts Cooperative Investment in a Human Social Network." PLoS ONE, 6 (3):e18338, 2011.

Holmes, Hannah. *The Well-Dressed Ape: A Natural History of Myself.* New York, NY: Random House, 2009.

Kirsch, P., Esslinger, C., Chen, Q., et al. "Oxytocin Modulates Neural Circuitry for Social Cognition and Fear in Humans." *Journal of Neuroscience,* 25 (49):11489–11493, 2005.

Kisilevsky, Barbara S., Hains, Sylvia M. J., Kang, Lee, et al. "Effects of Experience on Fetal Voice Recognition." *Psychological Science* 14 (3):220–224, 2003.

Krumhuber, Eva G., and Manstead, Antony S. R. "Can Duchenne Smiles Be Feigned? New Evidence on Felt and False Smiles." *Emotion,* Vol. 9(6):807–820, December 2009.

Ledo, Joseph. *The Emotional Brain: The Mysterious Underpinnings of Emotional Life*. New York, NY: Simon & Schuster, 1998.

Libet B., Gleason, C.A., Wright, E.W., and Pearl D. K. "Time of Conscious Intention to Act in Relation to Onset of Cerebral Activity (Readiness-Potential). The Unconscious Initiation of a Freely Voluntary Act." *Brain* 106 (Pt 3):623–642, September 1983.

Lewis, Thomas, Amini, Fari, and Lannon, Richard. *A General Theory of Love*. London, UK: Vintage, 2001

Myers, David G. *Intuition: Its Powers and Perils*. Newhaven, CT: Yale University Press, 2002.

Olson, Ingrid, and Marshuetz, Christy. *First Impressions of Beauty May Demonstrate Why the Pretty Prosper*. Philadelphia, PA: University of Pennsylvania, 2006.

Perry, Elaine K., Ashton, Heather, and Young, Allan H. *Neurochemistry of Consciousness: Neurotransmitters in Mind*. Amsterdam, Netherlands: John Benjamins Pub. Co., 2002

Pinker, Stephen. *How The Mind Works*. New York, NY: W. W. Norton & Company, 2009.

Rand, Ayn. *Philosophy: Who Needs It*. The Ayn Rand Library, Vol. 1. New York, NY: Signet Books, 1984.

Riesterer, Tim. "Stimulate Your Customer's Lizard Brain to Make a Sale." *Harvard Business Review, HBR Blog Network,* www.blogs.hbr.org/cs/2012/07/stimulate_your_customers_lizar.html, accessed July 31, 2012.

Rock, David. "SCARF: A Brain-Based Model for Collaborating with and Influencing Others." *NeuroLeadership Journal* 1: 1–9, 2008.

Ronson, Jon. *The Psychopath Test: A Journey Through the Madness Industry*. New York, NY: Riverhead Trade, 2012.

Rosenberg, Marshall. *Living Nonviolent Communication: Practical Tools to Connect and Communicate Skillfully in Every Situation*. Louisville, CO: Sounds True, 2012.

Ryan, Christopher, and Jethá, Cacilda. *Sex at Dawn: The Prehistoric Origins of Modern Sexuality*. New York, NY: Harper, 2010.

Sapolsky, Robert. "Human Behavioral Biology." Stanford University. Undergraduate biology course, 2011.

Shahani-Denning, Comila. "Physical Attractiveness Bias in Hiring: What Is Beautiful Is Good," www.hofstra.edu/pdf/orsp_shahani-denning_spring03.pdf, accessed November 05, 2012.

Shubin, Neil. *Your Inner Fish: A Journey into the 3.5-Billion-Year History of the Human Body.* London, UK: Vintage, 2009.

Sperry, Roger. "Bridging Science and Values: A Unifying View of Mind and Brain." *American Psychologist.* April 1977.

Stringer, Chris, and Andrews, Peter. *The Complete World of Human Evolution.* London, UK: Thames & Hudson, 2012.

Westermarck, Edvard. *The History of Human Marriage.* Ann Arbor, MI: University of Michigan Library, 1922.

About the Author

Born in England and living in Canada with his wife and two children, Mark Bowden is the creator of TRUTHPLANE™, a unique model of training for anyone whose success depends upon communication that builds strong and trusting relationships. His TRUTHPLANE™ communication system, based on his experience of over 20 years in performance and his own fascination and in-depth study of human interaction and the science of the living world, has garnered him a reputation for being one of the world's body language experts, top performance trainers, and a sought-after keynote speaker. He delivers speeches and seminars worldwide on persuasive and influential verbal and nonverbal language using communication structures that help you stand out, win trust, and profit. His communication techniques, in which he trains individuals and groups worldwide, are used by top executives and organizational and political leaders around the globe who want to gain an advantage beyond words when they communicate with everyone around them. His client list of leading businesspeople, teams, and politicians includes CEOs of Fortune 500 companies and leaders of G8 powers.

Mark's first and best-selling body language book, *Winning Body Language: Control the Conversation, Command Attention, and Convey the Right Message without Saying a Word* (McGraw Hill, 2010) has been translated into five languages and his second *Winning Body Language for Sales Professionals* is hot on its heels.

Mark can be contacted via www.truthplane.com.

Index